HIS NAME IS
STILL
MUDD

THE CASE AGAINST DOCTOR SAMUEL ALEXANDER MUDD

Edward Steers, Jr.

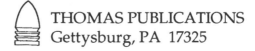

THOMAS PUBLICATIONS
Gettysburg, PA 17325

veritas praevalebit
(truth will prevail)

Copyright © 1997 Edward Steers, Jr.

Printed and bound in the United States of America

Published by THOMAS PUBLICATIONS
       P.O. Box 3031
       Gettysburg, Pa. 17325

ISBN-1-57747-019-2 (Softcover)
ISBN-1-57747-025-7 (Hardcover)

Cover design by Ryan C. Stouch

To Pat,

who has been cheerfully living with
Abraham Lincoln for these many years.

CONTENTS

Foreword v

Acknowledgements viii

Introduction 1

CHAPTERS

1 A horse thief points the way 4

2 Jefferson Davis says no 10

3 Sic semper tyrannis 21

4 Dr. Mudd tells his side of the story 28

5 Not quite the truth, the whole truth, and nothing but the truth 39

6 What did Mudd know and when did he know it? 49

7 The case against Dr. Mudd 60

8 We cannot escape history 70

9 The good doctor 82

10 Inter arma silent leges 89

APPENDICES

1 Statement of Samuel A. Mudd, voluntary statement, undated, in Mudd's own handwriting 106

2 Statement drafted by Col. H.H. Wells after the Friday, April 21, 1865, interrogation of Dr. Mudd 111

3 Andrew Johnson's pardon of Dr. Mudd 116

4 President Jimmy Carter's letter to Dr. Richard D. Mudd 118

5 President Ronald Reagan's letter to Dr. Richard D. Mudd 120

6 "Lost" statement of George A. Atzerodt 121

7 Affidavit of George W. Dutton concerning certain statements made by Dr. Samuel A. Mudd since his trial 125

8 Partial statement of Dr. Mudd in response to G.W. Dutton 127

9 Report of Lieutenant Alexander Lovett 129

10 Obituary of Samuel A. Mudd 131

11 The Samuel Mudd Relief Act of 1997 and H.R. 1885 134

Selected Bibliography 138

Notes 140

Index 158

FOREWORD

Historical myths fall into two general categories: those that spring up spontaneously and those that are manufactured. All three of the principal myths that grew out of the Lincoln assassination were manufactured:

1. That Secretary of War Edwin M. Stanton conspired with others to assassinate Lincoln,
2. That John Wilkes Booth escaped at the Garrett farm and died a suicide on January 13, 1903, under the alias David E. George, in a cheap hotel at Enid, Oklahoma Territory, and,
3. That Dr. Samuel A. Mudd was convicted in 1865 and sent to prison by a vengeful government only because he followed his Hippocratic oath and set the broken leg of John Wilkes Booth.

The fabrications that once supported the "Stanton was involved" myth have been utterly demolished in recent years by scholarly research; the "Booth escaped" myth, already in tatters, was reduced to nonsense by the testimony of expert witnesses in a 1995 civil suit in a Baltimore court. The third myth—that Dr. Samuel A. Mudd was "railroaded" into prison—continues to have life and attract support. It is this myth that Dr. Steers challenges in his carefully researched book.

The "Dr. Mudd was innocent" theme began to take shape in a book entitled *The Life of Dr. Samuel A. Mudd* by Nettie Mudd Monroe, published in 1906. Mrs. Monroe hardly knew her father. He died January 10, 1883, on Nettie's fifth birthday. However, she had many family papers available to her, as well as the recollections of her mother, Sarah Mudd, who lived on until 1911. The tone of later public relations efforts on Dr. Samuel A. Mudd's behalf was set in the last sentence of his son-in-law's introduction to Nettie's book. On April 14, 1906, D. Eldridge Monroe wrote:

> *Has not the time arrived to fully vindicate the name of Dr. Samuel A. Mudd, who was so cruelly and unjustly called upon to suffer—and to remove from that name the faintest shadow of doubt that may exist regarding his complicity in the great crime committed in Ford's Theatre, in Washington, forty-one years ago?*

In the late 1920s a young physician, Dr. Richard D. Mudd, began to interest himself in establishing the innocence of his grandfather, Dr. Samuel A. Mudd. His political and public relations efforts have been continuous, skillful, and effective. Over time, Dr. Richard D. Mudd developed a simple appeal, stated over and over and over and over again:

Dr. Samuel Mudd was a kindly country physician. He was arrested, tried, and convicted by a vengeful and hysterical government for the sole reason that he kept his Hippocratic oath and set the broken leg of John Wilkes Booth—a man he did not recognize. He was innocent of any complicity in the conspiracy.

This simplistic defense attracted conspiracy buffs and "true believers" looking for a cause. Dr. Samuel A. Mudd soon became fashionable, and promoting his innocence was worth votes to politicians without any bad side effects. It was not necessary to do any research or to read dreary testimony; just declare yourself in favor of exonerating the poor man, and then stand virtuously on the side of truth and justice.

For a good example of how this worked, the Michigan legislature adopted Concurrent Resolution No. 126 in July 1973. It followed almost precisely the routine used by Dr. Richard Mudd in his public relations campaign: a country doctor doing his bounden duty by setting the broken leg of a man who came to his door asking for professional help.

It was not until the Mudds pressured the Army Board for the Correction of Military Records to expunge the record of Dr. Mudd's conviction that things began to go sour. Researchers started reading the official transcript of the trial in the National Archives. Dr. Mudd, they learned, was not the saintly man depicted in Mudd propaganda. He had treated some of his slaves harshly, shooting one man—who survived—and flogging a young woman. More, he knew Booth and knew him well—actually Booth had been a guest in Mudd's home. He had been involved with Booth in a plan to capture Lincoln and carry him off to Richmond. Further, he had helped Booth to escape on April 15, knowing who he was and what he had done. Then he lied repeatedly to Federal investigators. In short, Dr. Mudd was guilty as set out in the specification in that he did "...advise, encourage, receive, entertain, harbor and conceal, aid and assist the said John Wilkes Booth...."

In 1992 the Army Board for the Correction of Military Records (ABCMR) recommended to the Secretary of the Army that he set aside the conviction on the ground that the military commission lacked jurisdiction to try Dr. Mudd. On July 22, 1992, this recommendation was denied by Acting Assistant Secretary of the Army William D. Clark who stated that it was not the role of the ABCMR to settle historical disputes or to act as an appellate court. The Mudds asked the new Secretary of the Army to review this decision. Assistant Secretary of the Army Sara E. Lister upheld Clark's decision on February 2, 1996, stating that: "Any further Army action would be an ill-advised attempt to alter legal history by non-judicial means. It would improperly disturb the importance of the finality of both judicial and executive decisions."

This would seem to have ended the matter. But no, the Mudd "innocence" machine is versatile if nothing else. Congressman Steny Hoyer of Maryland has introduced H. R. 1885, a bill which would order the Secretary of the Army to "set aside" the 1865 conviction of Dr. Samuel A. Mudd. Perhaps he is not serious but merely trolling for votes among the numerous Mudds, their kin, and followers in his congressional district. Still, it is incredible that Mr. Hoyer seems to believe that Congress can legislate innocence.

This book by Dr. Edward Steers, Jr. takes the reader through the complexities of the Dr. Samuel A. Mudd case with a sure hand and in an organized manner. For the very first time a respected Lincoln scholar has challenged the Mudd myth. It is about time.

James O. Hall
McLean, Virginia
July 22, 1997

ACKNOWLEDGEMENTS

Even as the body of Abraham Lincoln lay comatose in a rear bedroom of the Peterson house opposite Ford's Theatre, the government began to gather information about the terrible crime which John Wilkes Booth had just committed. Today, one hundred and thirty-two years later, the gathering and sifting of such information goes on, and occasionally new information is uncovered which adds light to the dark shadows surrounding Booth's act.

Among the many people who have spent untold hours researching the assassination of Abraham Lincoln, one person stands paramount. For over fifty years James O. Hall has searched the records and recorded the facts and myths which poured out of the Lincoln assassination, leaving not even the smallest pebble unturned in his search to understand every aspect of that momentous event. Today, every student and scholar in the field of the Lincoln assassination owes an enormous debt to James O. Hall. Much of what we know today about Lincoln's murder we learned from him. I am personally indebted to Mr. Hall for generously sharing his extensive files and scholarship with me, and for his thoughtful review of this work. If there is any failing or error in it, it is only because I failed to follow or inadvertently overlooked Mr. Hall's advice.

I would also like to acknowledge the invaluable assistance of Joan L. Chaconas, former president of the Surratt Society and Lincoln Group of the District of Columbia, for her review and editorial help with the manuscript. Joan Chaconas is a tremendous source of knowledge on the history of the District of Columbia and the events surrounding the assassination of Abraham Lincoln, and is always generous in her willingness to help find answers for those who have questions.

Finally I would like to acknowledge the staff and leadership of the Surratt Society, Surratt House Museum, and writers for the *Surratt Courier* (newsletter) for providing a wonderful resource from which students of the Lincoln assassination can continuously learn.

Introduction

In 1979, President Jimmy Carter wrote a letter to the grandson of Dr. Samuel A. Mudd[1] in which he stated:

> ...*I want to express my personal opinion that the declarations made by President Johnson[2] in pardoning Dr. Mudd substantially discredit the validity of the military commission's judgment.[3]*
>
> ...*A careful reading of the information provided to me about this case led to my personal agreement with the findings of President Johnson.[4] I am hopeful that these conclusions will be given widespread circulation which will restore dignity to your grandfather's name and clear the Mudd family name of any negative connotation or implied lack of honor.*

President Carter's hope that his letter would receive widespread circulation was realized. Simultaneous with Dr. Richard Mudd's receipt of it, Carter released his letter to the media through newsman Roger Mudd.[5] The media and the American public universally accepted Carter's letter as absolving Samuel Mudd of any wrongdoing or involvement in the horrendous murder of Abraham Lincoln by John Wilkes Booth.

Not to be outdone by his presidential counterpart, Ronald Reagan also wrote a letter eight years later to Richard Mudd expressing his personal belief that Samuel Mudd was, "...indeed innocent of any wrongdoing."[6]

In the intervening years since Samuel Mudd's pardon by Andrew Johnson and President Carter's letter, the perception of Dr. Mudd has become one of a simple country doctor who, in administering the Hippocratic oath, fell victim to a vengeful and hysterical government. That perception has been fueled by significant forces including Hollywood, television, the print media, and politicians. State legislatures[7] have passed resolutions exonerating Mudd and calling for the official reversal of the findings of the military tribunal that convicted and sentenced him. Efforts even exist for the issuance of a commemorative postal stamp honoring the doctor.

Much of the effort to rehabilitate Dr. Mudd has come from his grandson, Dr. Richard Dyer Mudd, who for over seventy years has waged a tireless battle to overturn the results of the military tribunal which convicted Dr. Mudd. Beginning with Franklin D. Roosevelt and ending with Jimmy Carter, Richard Mudd has petitioned every president on his grandfather's behalf.[8]

While successfully influencing public opinion, especially through the news media, Richard Mudd's efforts have fallen short of overturning his grandfather's conviction as an accomplice of John Wilkes Booth. President Carter, in his letter to Richard Mudd, astutely stated the reality of Mudd's situation when he wrote:

> *Regrettably, I am advised that the findings of guilt and the sentence of the military commission that tried Dr. Mudd in 1865 are binding and conclusive judgments, and that there is no authority under law by which I, as President, could set aside his conviction. All legal authority vested in the President to act in this case was exercised when President Johnson granted Dr. Mudd a full and unconditional pardon on February 8, 1869.*[9]

Samuel Mudd had been tried, convicted and sentenced by a military tribunal, and President Johnson's pardon established neither guilt nor innocence, but merely set Mudd free. Samuel Mudd in accepting President Johnson's pardon ended all recourse which he might have sought in pursuit of his claimed innocence.[10]

In his letter President Carter suggests that if any authority did exist in which he, as president, could set aside Samuel Mudd's conviction in 1865, he would do so. This is unfortunate, for both the legal authority of the military commission that tried Samuel Mudd, and its finding that Mudd was guilty as an accomplice of John Wilkes Booth, were correct.

Dr. Richard Dyer Mudd, grandson of Samuel A. Mudd, examining a jewel box made by Samuel A. Mudd while serving his prison sentence at Fort Jefferson.

Courtesy Dr. Richard D. Mudd.

While President Carter's letter (and subsequently President Reagan's) was a humanitarian expression intended to show sympathy for Dr. Samuel Mudd and his descendants' plight, it has no legal status nor was it intended to have legal status. And while Richard Mudd was greatly heartened by President Carter's expressions, they fell short of his lifelong effort to declare the military tribunal illegal, and declare his grandfather innocent of all wrongdoing.

While the majority of monographs and articles written about Samuel Mudd are universally in agreement of his innocence, there has not been enough discussion of the primary source materials which exist concerning the question of Mudd's complicity in the murder of Abraham Lincoln. While some of the evidence has had limited distribution, all of it is available to any individual who is willing to seek it.[11]

It is important to examine the wealth of evidence that exists within the writings and documents surrounding the events of Abraham Lincoln's murder so far as Dr. Samuel Alexander Mudd is concerned. The considerable bulk of information which has come to light over the past several years is primarily the result of one individual, James O. Hall. James Hall has proven to be an indefatigable researcher in pursuit of every detail associated with the murder of Abraham Lincoln. Equal to his tireless efforts in search of the truth is his boundless generosity in sharing his discoveries and extensive knowledge with any serious researcher. All any student of this tragedy need do is ask, and they shall receive. Few, if any, vocational historians have equaled the discoveries of James O. Hall in ferreting out the details related to Lincoln's murder.

Two of the principal myths of the Lincoln assassination must be challenged. First, that Dr. Samuel Alexander Mudd was an innocent victim stemming from his humanitarian efforts to render medical assistance to an injured man, and second, that the military tribunal which decided Mudd's fate was an illegal, rogue tribunal that unjustly punished him.

Presumably the individuals who reviewed Dr. Mudd's case and advised President Carter on his innocence in 1979 did not avail themselves of all of the historical materials nor of the several persons who are familiar with this evidence. This is not a criticism of those individuals, however, for much of the social consciousness of the nation has perceived Mudd's innocence for nearly a century. And while perception may be reality to most, it unfortunately belies the historical fact. His name is still Mudd.

1

A HORSE THIEF POINTS THE WAY.

John Fletcher's fears had been confirmed. He had warned the young man to return his rented horse by the supper hour, and now he was already several hours overdue. Fletcher had been troubled by the man's tardiness on previous occasions. When he had not returned by 10:30 p.m., Fletcher walked the short block from his stables to Pennsylvania Avenue to see if his overdue horse and rider were anywhere in sight. Incredibly, at that very moment, young Davy Herold was slowly making his way down Fifteenth Street toward the Avenue on Fletcher's horse.[1]

Four hours earlier, David Herold and three other men had met in a boarding house located just one block east of Ford's Theatre. There they reviewed their respective assignments one more time before setting out on their sinister plan. If each man carried out his murderous task according to plan, the president, vice-president and secretary of state would lie dead, leaving the nation in bloody disarray.

Herold had been assigned by the ring leader, John Wilkes Booth, to accompany Lewis Powell [alias Paine] to the home of Secretary of State William Seward. Herold would guard Powell's horse while he murdered the convalescing Seward.

Forcing his way into Seward's home, Powell made his way to Seward's bedroom where he proceeded to wreak his carnage. Frightened by the blood-chilling screams coming from the house, Herold abandoned Powell's horse, and galloped off in the direction of Fourteenth Street leaving the would-be assassin to fend for himself.

Fleeing the scene, Herold turned onto Pennsylvania Avenue where he came into Fletcher's view. Fletcher called out to Herold, demanding that he bring his horse back at once. The startled Herold pulled back on the reins, and spurring his mount, galloped down the Avenue and turned north onto Fourteenth Street with Fletcher running breathlessly in his wake. After racing a short block up Fourteenth Street, Herold turned east onto F

4

Street and headed at full gallop toward the Navy Yard Bridge according to a prearranged plan. It was approximately 10:30 p.m. on the night of April 14, 1865, the Good Friday preceding the Easter which would come to be known as *Black Easter*.

John Fletcher managed the stables owned by Thompson Naylor located on E Street just south of Pennsylvania Avenue. It was here that Davy Herold had rented the horse which he was now riding so vigorously into the night.

Only moments before, Fletcher had strolled up to the Union Hotel on Pennsylvania Avenue where he downed a glass of whiskey with another of his customers, a man named George A. Atzerodt. Fletcher thought Atzerodt a disheveled low-life who only recently frequented his stables together with his sidekick, Davy Herold. Atzerodt had stabled his own horse with Fletcher earlier in the day, calling for the horse around 10:00 p.m. Before riding off, Atzerodt asked Fletcher to join him in a drink, and the two men walked to the Union Hotel.

It seemed to Fletcher that Atzerodt was already "in his cups," and appeared wobbly from having spent most of the day in whiskey. After downing their drinks the two men parted. Fletcher gave little thought to the crazy German's remark that his spirited horse would be "...good upon the retreat" this particular night.[2]

Atzerodt had been assigned by Booth to assassinate Vice President Andrew Johnson who was resting in his room at the Kirkwood Hotel located at the corner of Twelfth Street and Pennsylvania Avenue. Earlier that same morning, Atzerodt had taken a room in the Kirkwood in anticipation of his bloody task. Still wobbly from alcohol, Atzerodt got as far as the hotel bar before his courage evaporated. Like Herold, Atzerodt fled his assigned task, and began wandering about the city at the very moment Herold was racing toward the Navy Yard Bridge.

Atzerodt was not Fletcher's problem however. The stable manager had to contend with getting his horse back from Davy Herold. Watching Herold turn east onto F Street, Fletcher turned and ran the few blocks back to his stables where he quickly saddled his own horse and set out after the fleeing thief. He remembered overhearing Atzerodt and Herold earlier, talking about a place called White Plains located across the Eastern Branch in Maryland and correctly assumed that Herold was headed in that direction. The city was fairly quiet except for the clatter of hoof beats which Fletcher noted as he raced past Tenth Street on his way toward the Navy Yard Bridge.

Riding hard, Fletcher arrived at the bridge located at the foot of Eleventh Street next to the Washington Navy Yard. He was stopped by the military pickets guarding the bridge who controlled all of the traffic into and out of the city. The bridge crossed the Eastern Branch of the Potomac River[3] connecting with a small settlement located on the eastern bank known as Uniontown. Sergeant Silas T. Cobb was in charge of the pickets on duty this night, and challenged Fletcher as he pulled up to the guard post out of breath.

The "Assassination" Conspirators.

John Wilkes Booth
Library of Congress

George Andrew Atzerodt
Library of Congress

Lewis Thornton Powell alias Lewis Paine (Payne).
Library of Congress

David E. Herold.
Library of Congress

Fletcher told Cobb his story of the stolen horse and asked if a young man had recently passed over the bridge. The sergeant told Fletcher that two men had recently passed over the bridge not minutes apart, the second man answering to Fletcher's description. Fletcher was sure the second man was Herold, and probably assumed the first man was his sidekick Atzerodt. Fletcher then asked Cobb for permission to cross over into Uniontown so that he might continue his pursuit of Herold and recover his stolen horse. As with the two before him, Cobb agreed to let Fletcher cross over, but told him he could not allow him to cross back before morning. Although the threat of a Confederate attack on Washington was no longer a reality, illegal trafficking into the city was. So, while there seemed no danger in letting someone leave, some control was still exercised over persons entering the city. A 9:00 p.m. curfew barring all unauthorized traffic into the city was still in effect. Those were Cobb's orders.[4]

Angered by the soldier's decision, and unable to stay away from his stables until morning, Fletcher wheeled his horse around, and rode back into the city returning to his stables on E Street.

Frustrated, Fletcher was not yet finished. After he stabled his horse he walked the short distance to police headquarters on Tenth Street where he reported the theft of his horse to the detective on duty. He was told that the police had picked up a stray horse near the Lincoln Hospital in southeast Washington, and had stabled it at the headquarters of the 22nd Army Corps commanded by Major General Christopher Columbus Augur.[5]

Accompanied by police detective Charles Stone, Fletcher walked over to the army headquarters a few blocks north. He was shown a saddle which he recognized as belonging to the disheveled little German whose name he momentarily forgot. He told Augur that he had the owner's name on a card back at his stables. Fletcher and Stone then returned to the stables to retrieve the card for General Augur. Written on the card was the name, *George A. Atzerodt.*

Fletcher was shown the horse which the police had brought in sometime around midnight. It was a large, brown horse distinguished by having lost one eye — the very same horse that Fletcher had saddled on many an occasion for the friendly Atzerodt. Fletcher must have been puzzled. The saddle was not on the horse Atzerodt had stabled only hours before, but Fletcher knew that the saddle belonged to the German. Still, he assumed that the two men that passed over the Navy Yard Bridge around eleven o'clock that evening were Davy Herold and his cohort, George Atzerodt.

Atzerodt, of course, had not passed over the bridge ahead of Davy Herold as Fletcher assumed.[6] That rider was John Wilkes Booth, fleeing his act of murder at Ford's Theatre only minutes before. Booth and Herold would shortly rendezvous at a prearranged location just over the District line where they planned to meet with Atzerodt and Lewis Powell. Unknown to Fletcher, it was Powell who had been riding the one-eyed horse whose owner was John Wilkes Booth.[7]

Important is the fact that Fletcher's information clearly linked Davy Herold to George Atzerodt, and within a matter of hours, Atzerodt, whose saddle was now in the custody of General Augur along with the stray, one-eyed horse, would be directly linked to John Wilkes Booth.[8]

Washington City's provost marshall, Major James O'Beirne, fearing a possible threat to Vice President Andrew Johnson's life, sent police detective John Lee to the Kirkwood Hotel, located at Twelfth and Pennsylvania Avenue, to guard him. Johnson, having relocated to Washington as a result of his election as vice president, had rented a room at the Kirkwood Hotel until he could find a suitable house.

When Lee arrived at the hotel on the evening of the 15th, he questioned the barkeeper and night clerk, a man named Michael Henry who, in the course of their discussions, told Lee that "a suspicious appearing character" had registered in Room 126 on the morning of April 14.[9] Lee proceeded to Room 126, and after forcing the door, searched the room. Among the items he found was a bankbook with the owner's name clearly written inside, *John Wilkes Booth*.[10] The "suspicious appearing character" that Lee referred to was George A. Atzerodt, Davy Herold's friend.

In less than twenty-four hours following the shooting of Lincoln, officials had a clear link between John Wilkes Booth and George Atzerodt, and thanks to John Fletcher, Augur linked George Atzerodt to David Herold. Augur had reason to believe that Herold and his friend had fled over the Navy Yard Bridge into southern Maryland. Who else might have fled over the bridge was uncertain for a time, but by mid-morning General Augur's staff came to believe the first bridge-crosser was Booth.

As a result of Fletcher's visit to army headquarters, Augur assembled a troop of the 13th New York Cavalry under the command of Lieutenant David D. Dana, and sent them over the Navy Yard Bridge and into southern Maryland. Shortly after noon on Saturday, April 15, Lieutenant Dana and his troopers arrived at the small village of Bryantown, some thirty miles southeast of Washington. Here they commandeered the local tavern and set up their headquarters.[11]

Fifteen hours after the assassination attempt at Ford's Theatre, Lieutenant Dana and the men of the 13th New York Cavalry were as close to the assassin Booth as any of the military would come over the next eleven days. Three miles to the north of Dana and his troopers, his broken leg now splinted, John Wilkes Booth was resting fitfully in the home of the good doctor, Samuel Alexander Mudd.

2

JEFFERSON DAVIS SAYS NO.

At what precise moment John Wilkes Booth decided to change his plans from one of capture to one of murder is not clear. The idea of capturing Lincoln was an old story—one that had a varied cast of characters including the nephew of a former president of the United States, and two officers of the Confederate States Army.[1]

Joseph Walker Taylor, a major in the Confederate Army, was the architect of one of the earliest plots to capture Lincoln. Walker Taylor, as he was known to his friends, was well connected in all respects. A Kentuckian like Lincoln, Taylor was the nephew of former president Zachary Taylor, and first cousin to Major General Richard Taylor, C.S.A., who was in command of the District of West Louisiana.[2] More importantly, he was first cousin to Sarah Knox Taylor, daughter of President Zachary Taylor, and the first wife of Confederate President Jefferson Davis.

Walker Taylor was on the staff of General Simon Bolivar Buckner who was stationed at Fort Donelson in western Tennessee in 1862. When Ulysses S. Grant successfully encircled Fort Donelson, Buckner was given command of the post so that he could surrender it to Grant.[3] While Buckner was forced to accept Grant's "unconditional surrender" terms, Walker Taylor had other plans. Wounded in the cheek and neck, Taylor decided to join forces with Nathan Bedford Forrest and successfully slip out of the fort the night before its surrender, then make his way to Louisville where he began a convalescence from his wounds.

As his health steadily improved, Taylor decided to make a clandestine visit to Washington, D. C. where he stayed with his uncle, Union Brigadier General Joseph Taylor, brother of Zachary Taylor. Young Taylor knew that he would not be betrayed by his elderly uncle. Like many families, the Taylors had members serving on both sides of the conflict. Walker Taylor was one of four brothers with divided allegiance; two were officers in the Union army while two served as officers in the Confederate army.

While convalescing in Washington, Taylor boldly attended a White House reception where he was introduced to the president. Lincoln, noticing Taylor's wounds, asked in what battle he had been wounded. When Taylor replied, "Fort Donelson," Lincoln commended Taylor for the great victory, and bravery of the Union forces in the fort's capture.[4] The smile that must have crossed Taylor's face can only be imagined.

After several days of observing Lincoln's daily routine, Taylor hatched his plot to capture the president, and take him south to Richmond where he would become a bargaining chip in negotiating prisoner exchange. While Taylor believed his plan was certain to succeed, he felt protocol required that he receive the approval of President Davis which he felt confident he would get.

According to Colonel William Preston Johnston, Davis's aide-de-camp,[5] Taylor traveled from Washington to Richmond in the summer of 1862 where he joined Davis and Johnston for breakfast at the Confederate White House. During the course of their meeting Taylor outlined his plan to capture Lincoln one evening while the president made his routine trip to his summer quarters at Soldiers' Home in the northern part of the city.[6]

Taylor's plan was simple:

> Lincoln does not leave the White House until evening, or near twilight, and then with only a driver, he takes a lonely ride two or three miles in the country to a place called Soldiers' Home, which is his summer residence. My point is to collect several of these Kentuckians whom I see about here doing nothing and who are brave enough for such a thing as that, and capture Lincoln, run him down the Potomac, and cross him over just where I crossed, and the next day will have him here.[7]

Davis listened intently before responding to Taylor's scheme. "No sir, I will not give my authority to abduct Lincoln," Davis said pointedly.[8] He did not believe such a plan could be successfully carried out without the high probability of Lincoln being killed. Davis' answer to Taylor was direct:

> I suppose Lincoln is a man of courage. ...He would undoubtedly resist being captured. ...I could not stand the imputation of having consented to let Mr. Lincoln be assassinated.[9]

Of course, Davis was right. In any attempt to capture the president of the United States, the probability that the president or, for that matter, someone else close to the president, would be killed was extremely high. Davis put an immediate end to Taylor's plan to capture Lincoln.

In 1889, only weeks before his death, Davis wrote to Taylor asking him to record the details of his proposal together with his (Davis') refusal to sanction such a plot.[10] Davis wanted to use Taylor's statement to blunt recurring inferences that Davis was somehow involved or sanctioned Booth's

Jefferson Davis.

Abraham Lincoln.
Last known photograph
taken on March 6, 1865 by
Henry F. Warren on the
White House balcony.

successful attempt in 1865. While Davis may have prevented the possible killing of Lincoln in 1862, there are some today who feel that circumstantial evidence clearly points to his full knowledge, and even acquiescence in Booth's eventual murder of Lincoln three years later.[11]

By the summer of 1864, the military situation had changed dramatically. Any illusions of a short war with Confederate success had completely faded away. Although some felt uneasy about Lincoln's chances for re-election in the fall, stunning Union victories at Atlanta, and later in the Shenandoah Valley would insure four more years with Lincoln as president.[12] Any hope of a negotiated peace with the "tyrant in the White House" was beyond reach.

During the early spring of 1864, Colonel Bradley T. Johnson (soon to be promoted to brigadier general), a native of Frederick, Maryland, and officer in the Confederate army, disclosed his own daring plan to capture Lincoln. Johnson's plan had all the earmarks of success. Johnson was serving under the command of Major General Wade Hampton[13] when he was ordered to join Major General Jubal A. Early's army in the upper Shenandoah Valley. Johnson proposed his idea of capturing Lincoln to Hampton who, according to Johnson, gave his approval.[14] As with Taylor in 1862, it is unreasonable to believe that Johnson and Hampton would plan to carry out the capture operation without first clearing it with Confederate authorities, including Jefferson Davis. Before Johnson could begin implementation of his plan, however, he was ordered to take his Maryland brigade and join Early, as a part of Early's Army of the Valley.

Like Walker Taylor before him, Johnson saw the vulnerability of the summer White House. Johnson had proposed picking two hundred of his best men and horses, and after crossing the Potomac River into Maryland at White's Ford,[15] heading for the Soldiers' Home located three miles north of the White House. Here, at Soldiers' Home, Lincoln had established his summer residence in Anderson Cottage.[16] The Lincoln and the Stanton families had taken advantage of the cooler setting at Soldiers' Home in order to flee the disease-ridden summer months in Washington.

Lincoln was often accompanied to and from the Home by a detachment of cavalry which provided a modest guard. Occasionally, however, Lincoln would make the short ride alone much to the consternation of those concerned about his safety. Cavalry guard or not, a contingent of two hundred battle-hardened Confederate cavalrymen could easily overwhelm any guard and capture Lincoln.

Johnson's plan was to raid the Soldiers' Home one evening, capture Lincoln, and with five selected troopers send him east, then south over the Eastern Branch of the Potomac River into southern Maryland following the well-known route of the Confederate Secret Service. This plan and route closely resembled that of another would-be kidnapper, John Wilkes Booth.

Brigadier General Bradley T. Johnson, C.S.A.

View of Soldiers' Home, Scott Hall on right of picture, Anderson Cottage on left of picture. From a stereo card ca. 1866.

As the select party of five headed toward southern Maryland with their incredible prize, Johnson would take his remaining troopers, and retrace his steps west toward the Potomac recrossing the river at White's Ford, Point of Rocks, Shepherdstown or Williamsport depending on the enemy's response. Johnson was convinced that his large raiding party would draw the Federals away from the real quarry which would then allow them to safely slip through the thin Union lines and over the Potomac River into Virginia. It was a well thought out plan which had a high probability for success.

Reporting to Early, recently victorious over Major General David Hunter in the Upper Valley, Johnson outlined his plan (and Hampton's previous approval) to the irascible general. Early, readying his army for a daring attack on Washington, put Johnson on hold by telling him to forget any plans to raid Soldiers' Home until after the upcoming campaign.

Although Early failed in his bold attempt to enter Washington and sack the city, the Confederate effort sufficiently scared Washington to force Grant to respond with considerable force. Grant organized a new army, designated the Army of the Shenandoah, under Major General Philip Sheridan, and ordered it to eliminate all organized Confederate resistance in the Shenandoah Valley, and to lay waste to the considerable supplies in the valley which continued to feed Lee's Army of Northern Virginia.

The ultimate outcome of this effort by Union forces was the destruction of Early's army and the removal of Early from Confederate command. This ended any scheme of Johnson's to capture Lincoln, but by the time Early and Johnson were knocked out of the war in December 1864, John Wilkes Booth was well on his way to upstaging all other plans to capture the Union president.

Shortly past midnight on the evening of March 15, 1865, John Wilkes Booth and six of his cohorts rendezvoused at a popular restaurant only a few blocks from Ford's Theatre.[17] The group had gathered at Booth's command ostensibly to review their plan to capture the president. Once captured, the details of the escape were well laid out. It was the act of capturing Lincoln that was problematic to some members of Booth's cadre of compatriots.

There was dissension among the band of conspirators. Booth's familiarity and easy access to Ford's Theatre led him to favor it as the site for abduction. Lincoln was known to frequent the theater. To some in the group, capturing Lincoln from the theater was fraught with difficulty, and too easily prone to failure, and failure meant disaster. It would be better to pick off the president on one of his many trips about the city, especially his trips to and from Soldiers' Home. The problem with Soldiers' Home, however, was that the Lincoln family did not set up residence there until late spring which was several weeks away. Time was working against the conspirators and an ominous feeling had overtaken some in the group that the longer the delay the more likely they would be discovered. If they were to strike it had better be soon.[18]

Fortunately the opportunity presented itself within hours of the midnight meeting. The following day, March 16, Booth learned from fellow actor E. L. Davenport, that Lincoln would visit the Campbell Hospital on the northern outskirts of the District on the 17th to witness a play for the benefit of convalescing soldiers. Booth's contacts allowed him easy access to such information and his presence at such an event would be commonplace, arousing no suspicion.

Word went out to the anxious conspirators, to assemble in readiness for execution of their assigned roles. When Lincoln left the hospital to return to the White House following the performance, his carriage would be overtaken, and he would be spirited away, over the well-established escape route through southern Maryland, and over the Potomac River into Virginia. Once over the river, the safety of Richmond would be close at hand.

To the conspirators' chagrin, however, their plot failed when Lincoln changed his plans at the last minute in order to meet with a contingent of soldiers, and accept a captured Confederate battle flag as a token of Union victory.[19] To add salt to Booth's already festering wounds, Lincoln greeted the regiment from the balcony of the National Hotel on Pennsylvania Avenue, where Booth had made his residence on that very day.[20]

The abortive attempt on March 17 was the last straw for two of the conspirators. For Arnold and O'Laughlen, Booth's scheme was increasingly hapless. Fraught with danger from the outset, it appeared to the two Baltimore school chums to be too risky to warrant the effort. To Arnold and O'Laughlen, capture was not only risky, it required the careful coordination of too many people whose enthusiasm was increasingly suspect.

Contrary to some historical accounts, Booth did not hatch his plan to murder Lincoln on the morning of April 14. It was at some point between the failed capture attempt on March 17 and April 12 that Booth decided on assassination. We know this because by Wednesday, April 12, George Atzerodt was selling Booth's carriage and Lewis Powell was scouting the Seward House[21] familiarizing himself with its layout and the location of the bedridden Seward.[22] It appears that Seward was already a target, and Powell was the designated assassin.

Booth had gone to the National Theatre on April 13 to see if Lincoln was planning on visiting the theater that evening. On the morning of the 14th, George Atzerodt registered at the Kirkwood Hotel located at the corner of Twelfth Street and Pennsylvania Avenue. There, Vice President Andrew Johnson was living in a room only a few steps from where Atzerodt set up his own housekeeping.[23]

At what precise moment Booth knew of Lincoln's planned visit to Ford's Theatre on Friday evening is not clear. It is also not clear at what moment

Mary Lincoln decided that she and her husband would attend the theater Friday evening, and whether news of their visit somehow passed from the White House eventually reaching Booth. While Booth and several of his cohorts were active on Wednesday, April 12, it may have been in anticipation of a future visit not yet planned, or it may have been that word had leaked that Mrs. Lincoln was contemplating a theater visit in hopes of gaining an earned respite for her war-weary husband. In any event, sinister movements were underway.

On April 13 Booth paid a visit to the National Theatre on Pennsylvania Avenue, another favorite spot of Lincoln's. Ostensibly, Booth was trying to find out if Lincoln would be attending the performance there. On the morning of the 14th, he visited Ford's Theatre to pick up his mail. He met with Harry Clay Ford,[24] who managed the theater's daily operation. Ford confirmed that both Lincoln and Grant would attend the evening performance. Of course, the presidential box would be reserved for the illustrious guests of the Ford brothers.[25]

That evening, the popular American actress, Laura Keene, was performing in the British comedy entitled, *Our American Cousin*. The performance was a benefit for the popular female star in which she would receive the proceeds of the evening receipts as her pay as one of the star performers at Ford's. The performance was sold out and Booth, ever the dramatic thespian, would himself play to a standing room only crowd for what he believed would be his greatest performance.

There is reason to believe that John Wilkes Booth became involved in Confederate underground activities as early as the spring of 1863. Booth was originally involved in smuggling drugs (quinine in particular) south. By late summer 1864, several war measures were instituted which dramatically changed both the demeanor and strategy of the conflict.

Among Ulysses S. Grant's first moves as general-in-chief in March 1864 was his suspension of prisoner exchange. By not exchanging captured soldiers Grant was in effect instituting a policy of strangling the Confederate war machine. While the North had substantial reserves of manpower to draw upon, the South did not. Suspension of prisoner exchange meant that the already undersized armies of the Confederacy could only get smaller. The Northern strategists knew that such depletion of manpower would eventually hurt the Confederacy. The down side, of course, was that Northern prisoners had to survive in Southern prison camps under conditions of extreme deprivation as the Confederacy slowly ran out of food, medical supplies, and facilities to support even a substandard existence. The result of having to provide for Northern prisoners of war only added further strain on a Confederate supply system that was already failing. On the other hand, the North had to care for increasing numbers of captured Confederates, putting an ever increasing strain on their resources.

As conditions deteriorated further, Northern prisoners suffered dispro-
portionately under dwindling Confederate resources causing increasing protests in the North. In August 1864, Secretary of War Edwin McMasters
Stanton issued a "retaliation order" in which rations for Southern prisoners
of war were reduced to levels believed commensurate with those issued to
Northern prisoners of war. The result was brutal on both sides. Booth, of
course, focused only on the condition of Southern prisoners of war and his
anger and hatred for Lincoln only grew more virulent.

Forty months into the war conditions had changed dramatically. Chiv-
alry and noble causes were rapidly crashing into a nightmare of devasta-
tion and brutality. To John Wilkes Booth, this was entirely the fault of
Union tyranny under the iron fist of the country's despotic Caesar, Abraham
Lincoln.

Booth's solution to the growing disaster facing the Confederacy was
actually quite reasonable from a strategic point of view and, if successful,
could prove of considerable help to the dying Confederacy. Booth, as several before him, proposed to capture Lincoln and take him to Richmond
where the authorities (Jefferson Davis) could force an exchange of Southern
prisoners for the Northern commander-in-chief. How many soldiers is a
president worth? Certainly a division and perhaps all of the divisions in
Union hands. Perhaps even a negotiated peace settlement.[26]

Walker Taylor, Bradley T. Johnson and John Wilkes Booth all proposed
to capture Abraham Lincoln, Commander-in-Chief of the United States
military forces as a military strategy to affect the outcome of the war. This
point should not be lost when discussing the Lincoln assassination story.
While kidnapping was a misdemeanor in 1865, capturing the commander-
in-chief was a military (war) action and fell under the jurisdiction of the
military. Virtually all of the plots against Lincoln were for the purpose of
affecting the outcome of the war, i.e. the military operations of the North.
Neither Taylor nor Johnson nor Booth had any personal designs in dealing
with a captured Lincoln. All of their efforts had but one objective, to affect
the military operations of the North.[27] It is also revealing that Taylor and
Jefferson Davis used the word "capture" in referring to Taylor's plot against
Lincoln.[28]

Whether Booth was even aware of prior plots to capture Lincoln such
as Walker Taylor's or Bradley T. Johnson's is unclear, but certainly it is not
unreasonable to believe that he had gotten wind of them at one point or
another. Some writers have even suggested that Booth, along with Atzerodt,
Arnold and O'Laughlen, simply rolled over from Bradley T. Johnson's plot
in the summer of 1864.[29] One thing is strikingly similar among all of the
proposals to capture Lincoln: the route of escape.

Throughout the war the Confederacy operated a clandestine secret service or underground which was officially within the Confederate Signal

The "Capture" Conspirators.

Michael O'Laughlen

Samuel Bland Arnold

John H. Surratt, Jr.

Edman Spangler

Service or, more accurately, Signal Bureau. Movement from the Confederacy into Maryland and Washington, D.C. was carried out over two principal routes; both were well laid out and staffed with Confederate agents. The principal route into Washington crossed the Potomac River from Mathias Point in King George County, Virginia to Allen's Fresh, Newport, Bryantown (Bryan Town), Surratt's Tavern and Washington.

According to a Confederate Signal Bureau document located in the National Archives[30], the Surratt Tavern was a specific stop along the underground route into the District of Columbia. At the time the document was written, the widowed Mary Surratt was operating the tavern and had not yet relocated her family to her house at 541 H Street in Washington. Her son, John Harrison Surratt, Jr., was serving as a Confederate courier and frequently traveled the route between Richmond and Washington carrying messages for the Confederate government. Mary was certainly aware of her son's activity and could not help but know that her tavern (and later boarding house) were Confederate safe houses.

The routes used by the Confederacy were for the safe conduct of "...letters, papers and light packages to the Dept." as well as for the safe conduct of people. It was this "safe route" through southern Maryland into Virginia that John Wilkes Booth had reconnoitered on several occasions in preparation for taking Lincoln to Richmond after his capture. To carry out such a plan required help, both directly in committing the act, and indirectly in assisting the safe transport south. Booth found a ready and willing cadre of individuals in developing his bold plan.

Booth needed two types of accomplices: those who would assist in the actual capture and those who would assist in facilitating the escape to Richmond.[31] These two groups were quite different in character. The first was put together as a tight conspiracy by Booth specifically for the purpose of capturing Lincoln while the second was already in place serving the Confederacy in a different role. Booth needed to tap into the second to assure the success of the first. He was able to do both which resulted in a very broad conspiracy across different organizational lines.

Among the first group, or inner circle, were Samuel Arnold, George Atzerodt, Davy Herold, Michael O'Laughlen, Lewis Powell, John Surratt and, of course, John Wilkes Booth.

Among the second group were a few who had knowledge of the plan to capture Lincoln and were prepared to aid in the flight to Richmond. Before his death twelve days after Lincoln's demise, over two dozen individuals would knowingly aid and abet the assassin of Abraham Lincoln. Dr. Samuel Alexander Mudd was well connected with his feet in both of these two camps.

3

SIC SEMPER TYRANNIS[1]

Sometime between 6:30 and 7:30 on Friday evening, April 14, John Wilkes Booth met with George Atzerodt, Louis Powell and Davy Herold in Powell's room at the boarding house of Mrs. Murphy.[2] Also known as the Herndon House, Mrs. Murphy's boarding house was located at the corner of Ninth and F Streets just one block from Ford's Theatre. Booth had arranged for Powell to stay there out of sight, to avoid any problems which might jeopardize his plans. It was here that the four conspirators met to go over their plan for the last time. Booth reviewed the role of each of the four men and each of their targets.[3]

Powell, along with Davy Herold as guide, would go to the home of William Seward to kill the secretary of state. Atzerodt, already registered in Room 126 at the Kirkwood Hotel, would call on Andrew Johnson and kill the vice president. Booth would take care of Lincoln.[4]

All was coordinated to take place at approximately 10:30 p.m. The four would then head across the Navy Yard Bridge and rendezvous just over the District line in Maryland at a spot known as Soper's Hill.[5]

After going over their plans one more time the four men melted into the surrounding neighborhood and waited until the assigned hour. As 10:00 p.m. approached all four assassins were within striking distance of their targets. Atzerodt, after leaving John Fletcher at the Union Hotel rode the two short blocks to the Kirkwood Hotel where he entered the bar for yet another swill of whiskey. Within a few feet of Andrew Johnson's room, Atzerodt's courage failed and he quickly left the hotel, mounted his horse and rode away.

At the moment Atzerodt's courage evaporated, Lewis Powell had talked his way into Seward's house located on Lafayette Square directly opposite the White House. Powell insisted that he hand-deliver a doctor's prescription to the bedridden Seward. Forcing his way into the house, Powell erupted in a rage and began attacking anyone who got in his way. Herold, waiting outside with Powell's horse, panicked on hearing the horrible screams coming from the house and, dropping the horse's reins, galloped off leaving Powell to fend for himself in escaping from the city. Powell's horse, owned by John Wilkes Booth, was characterized by having lost an eye.[6]

Booth, perhaps uncertain as to the resolve of his three cohorts, had no reservations as to his own. Arriving at the rear of the theater, he dismounted from his horse and called for Edman Spangler to hold the reins for the few minutes that he would be in the theater.[7] Spangler, working as a stagehand that evening, had his own work moving scene flats between acts. Spangler passed the reins of Booth's horse on to a young theater hand named "Peanuts" Burroughs.[8]

Once inside the rear door, Booth lifted a trap door set in the floor of the theater and made his way down a small set of stairs to the dug out cellar beneath the stage. Crossing beneath the stage area, he made his way up a second set of stairs and through another trap door which brought him to the opposite side of the back stage area. Here a door led into a small alley separating the theater from the Star Saloon which was immediately adjacent to the theater. By this manuever, Booth was able to pass from the rear of the theater to the front sidewalk on Tenth Street, leaving his horse carefully tended outside the rear door of the theater. Entering the saloon, he downed a brandy marking the time, and after a brief exchange with the barkeep slipped out the front of the saloon and entered the theater lobby through its front door.

A star figure of national renown, Booth had liberal access to the theater and its environs. Passing across the lobby, Booth climbed the stairs located on the left, and arriving at the area known as the dress circle, slowly made his way across the rear of the circle to the boxes located at the far end. Here the president and his party were enjoying the play being carried out on the stage directly below the two boxes.[9]

As Booth approached the outer door to the president's box he encountered Lincoln's personal valet and attendant, Charles Forbes.[10] After a brief exchange in which Booth presented Forbes with a card,[11] he entered the outer vestibule of the two boxes. Seated immediately inside the inner door were the president, Mrs. Lincoln, Major Henry Rathbone and his fiancee, Clara Harris.

Booth secured the outer door from any unexpected interruption by wedging a piece of wood, which he had previously hidden behind the door, between the door and the notch in the wall which he had carefully fashioned earlier in the day. With the outer door firmly secured, Booth slowly opened the inner door leading into the box where Lincoln and his companions were sitting. Raising his small derringer, he fired point-blank into the back of Lincoln's head.

Upper left: John T. Ford. Upper right: Harry Clay Ford.
Lower left: Laura Keene. Lower right: Ford's Theatre.

Major Henry Rathbone and his fiancee Clara Harris had accompanied President and Mrs. Lincoln to the theater and were sitting near them in the presidential box. On hearing the shot and Booth's dramatic shout of *Sic semper tyrannis*,[12] Rathbone jumped to his feet and attempted to subdue the assassin. Severely wounding Rathbone with his knife, Booth swung his legs over the balustrade and dropped to the stage ten feet below. Legend has Booth catching his spur in a flag of the Treasury Guard which was mounted vertically between the boxes. Other accounts of the time mention Booth catching his spur in the "National Standard." Both balustrades of the two boxes were covered with American flags at the time, and it seems more probable that Booth caught his spur in one of them as he swung his legs over the balustrade and dropped awkwardly to the stage below.[13]

Whichever flag ensnared Booth, it caused him to land off balance and resulted in a clean break of the fibula above the ankle in his left leg. The break did not effect the tibia, or weight-bearing bone. Although Booth was hurting, he remained quite mobile.[14]

Making his way across the stage, Booth dashed out of the rear door to his waiting horse still being cared for by young "Peanuts" Burroughs. Within minutes he was racing toward the Navy Yard Bridge and his first major hurdle in escaping the city and the authorities who were in a state of complete disorganization during the first minutes following the assassination.

Arriving at the Navy Yard Bridge at approximately 10:45 p.m., Booth was challenged by the guard, Sergeant Silas T. Cobb. Cobb questioned Booth briefly, and surprisingly, Booth not only gave his correct name, but also his correct destination. He said he was headed for Beantown located in southern Maryland.[15] Booth was not wearing a disguise.

Satisfied that Booth posed no threat to the army or the city, the unsuspecting sentry waved the killer across the bridge, sending him into the comparative safety of pro-Confederate southern Maryland. Booth's admitted destination of Beantown suggests that he was headed for the home of Dr. Mudd.[16]

Within minutes after Booth passed the sentries, a second rider arrived at the bridge. He too was challenged by Cobb, but unlike the first rider gave a false name. Also unlike the first rider, he gave a false destination. He also gave a false reason why he had overstayed his visit in the city, arriving at the bridge long after the curfew of 9:00 p.m. Davy Herold told Sergeant Cobb that he had been with a woman and had lost track of the time. Cobb seemed understanding. Certainly Herold's excuse seemed plausible. Like the first rider, Herold posed no threat leaving the city, and was waved across the bridge.[17]

Minutes later a third rider approached. As with the previous two, the rider was stopped. He gave his name as John Fletcher, and he told the guard that his purpose in crossing over the bridge was to recover his stolen

The Assassin's Targets.

Abraham Lincoln

Vice-President Andrew Johnson

Secretary of State William H. Seward

Ulysses S. Grant

horse from the thief Davy Herold. Cobb acknowledged that a man meeting Herold's description had passed over the bridge only minutes before, but said that if he allowed Fletcher to pass over the bridge he could not return until morning. Those were Cobb's orders and Fletcher could take them or leave them. Fletcher reluctantly chose to return to the city and seek another remedy to recover his stolen horse. As he wheeled his horse around and headed back into the city, the two horsemen were galloping as fast as their mounts would carry them up the road that ran between two of the forts which guarded the city from hostile forces.[18]

Sometime around 11:00 p.m., John Wilkes Booth and Davy Herold had passed into the relative safety of southern Maryland. Back in the city pandemonium reigned. By the time Secretary of War Edwin Stanton assumed effective control of the situation, Booth and Herold were approaching the tavern at Surrattsville well beyond the immediate grasp of the authorities. John Wilkes Booth had struck a daring and devastating blow against the United States and had won, or so it seemed.

It was close to midnight when the two fugitives made their stop at the crossroads tavern named for John Surratt. John Harrison Surratt, Sr. had died two and a half years earlier and his widow Mary had leased the tavern in the fall of 1864 to a man named John M. Lloyd.[19] The tavern, through the connection of John H. Surratt, Jr., was a "safe house" along the Confederate underground route from Richmond to Washington.[20]

Mary's ownership of the tavern, her son's role as one of Booth's conspirators, and the devastating testimony of John M. Lloyd, the tavern manager, all combined to send the woman to the gallows. Mary Surratt thus achieved the dubious distinction of becoming the first woman to be hanged by the United States Government.[21]

Arriving at the tavern, Herold dismounted and called for the manager, John Lloyd. After what seemed several minutes, an inebriated Lloyd came to the tavern door. Herold, irritated at Lloyd's delay in answering the door and sensing his inebriation, told him, "For God's sake Lloyd, make haste and get those things!"[22] Lloyd knew exactly what things he was to get without being told. He returned in a few minutes with two Spencer carbines, ammunition, the field glasses Mary Surratt had brought that day, and whiskey.[23] Due to the broken bone in Booth's leg, he had trouble balancing himself on his horse, and was unable to carry the second carbine. He told Lloyd to keep it.[24] Herold took the other carbine and passed the whiskey to Booth. After fortifying themselves with alcohol, the two men wheeled their horses about and galloped off with Booth telling Lloyd, "We have assassinated the President and Secretary Seward."[25]

Mary E. Surratt

The Surratt Boarding House

Surratt House and Tavern

4

DR. MUDD TELLS HIS SIDE OF THE STORY.

Situated approximately fifteen miles south of Mary Surratt's tavern was the home of Dr. Samuel Alexander Mudd. Mudd, a country physician who maintained a modest tobacco farm, was well known among the citizenry of Charles County, Maryland. He lived in a large, frame farmhouse with his wife Sarah Frances Dyer, affectionately known as "Frank," and their four young children.

According to statements given by Dr. Mudd,[1] it was around 4:00 a.m. when he and his wife were abruptly awakened from their sleep by a pounding on their front door. Mudd was alarmed at the loud banging at such an early hour and initially feared that it was someone or some persons up to no good.[2]

After briefly conferring with his wife as to who should go to the door, Dr. Mudd decided to go himself. He found two men outside his door, one man sitting astride a horse while the other man stood holding the reins of the two horses. Mudd claimed not to recognize the duo. On inquiring as to who they were and what they wanted, he was told they were "two strangers from St. Mary's Co. who were on their way to Washington. While enroute the horse of the mounted man had fallen, and broken the rider's leg."[3]

Mudd satisfied himself that one of the riders was indeed in distress and appeared to need medical assistance. He opened the door and invited the two men into his parlor, laying the injured man on a sofa. Mudd then obtained a light and, after examining the injured man's leg, helped him upstairs where he laid him in a bed and proceeded to treat him. Even in the better light of the bedroom Mudd still claimed not to recognize either of his two guests.

The uninjured man urged Mudd to attend to the injury of his friend quickly so that they could continue on their journey to Washington. In order to examine the injured man more thoroughly, Mudd had to cut the man's boot from his leg and foot "longitudinally in front of the instep." Removing the boot, Mudd set it aside. After examining the injured man's leg, he concluded that, "...there was one bone broken about two inches above the ankle joint—what we call a 'direct fracture.'" The injury was not compound, and Mudd proceeded to set the fracture and splint the leg using an old band box which he cut up and fashioned into a splint.

With the injured man treated and resting in the upstairs bedroom, Mudd walked around his farmyard giving instructions to the hired help before returning to the house for breakfast.[4]

The young man accompanying the injured man was "knocking about" and Dr. Mudd invited him to join him in breakfast. The "talkative" young man, according to Mudd, gave his name as Henson (Herold) and his friend's name as either Tyser or Tyson (Booth), Mudd could not be sure which. The two men, Mudd told his interrogators, **were complete strangers and he did not recognize either of them.** [Emphasis added].

As the two men finished their breakfast, Mr. Henson (Herold) asked Dr. Mudd if he could borrow a razor as his friend felt that he might feel better if he shaved off his moustache. In his written statements Dr. Mudd insisted that the injured man, Mr. Tyser, (Booth) had long chin whiskers and a moustache when he first examined him. Complying with Mr. Henson's (Herold) request, Mudd provided the injured man with one of his razors.

After finishing his dinner (the noonday meal) later that day, Mudd looked in on the injured man and noticed that he had indeed shaved off his moustache, but had retained his lengthy chin whiskers. A short while later, Mudd's wife would inform the doctor of a rather remarkable observation. She noticed that the chin whiskers had become detached when the man (Booth) came down the stairs later that afternoon.[5]

Following the noontime meal, Dr. Mudd and Mr. Henson (Herold) rode over to Oak Hill, the farm of Mudd's father. Henry Lowe Mudd, Sr. lived a short distance to the southeast of Samuel Mudd's farm. Mudd had taken Henson (Herold) to his father's farm to see if he might obtain a carriage or wagon to transport the injured Mr. Tyser (Booth). Arriving at the farm, Mudd found his father away, but met his brother there. No carriage or wagon was available or fit for serious service so Mr. Henson (Herold) told Mudd that he would ride into Bryantown and try and find a wagon.[6] Mudd agreed to accompany Mr. Henson (Herold) into town, for he had several errands of his own to run. Bryantown was a small village located approximately five miles south of Mudd's farm.

Henson (Herold), whose horse was considerably more sprightly than Mudd's, soon outran the doctor by some distance. As they approached Bryantown, Henson (Herold) abruptly reversed himself and rode back to Mudd exclaiming, "I believe I will get my friend to go to Rev. Wilmer's on horseback."[7]

According to Mudd's statement, the young man then galloped off in the direction of Mudd's house. Mudd continued on into Bryantown where he claimed to have purchased several needed items including nails, calico cloth, and pepper for which he paid cash. It was while attending to his shopping in Bryantown that Dr. Mudd admitted first hearing the news of Lincoln's murder. He did not, however, state if he had also learned who the murderer was.[8]

On his return from Bryantown, Mudd stopped by the home of one of his neighbors, Francis Farrell. Here he found another neighbor, John F. Hardy. The men met by the front gate where Mudd told them of Lincoln's assassination, as well as that of Seward and Seward's son, Frederick.[9] According to Farrell,[10] on learning of Lincoln's murder, he asked Mudd who had assassinated the President. Farrell stated that Mudd told him, "A man by the name of Booth." Hardy then asked if the assassin was the same Booth who had been in the area last fall. Mudd stated that he did not know—that there were three or four men named Booth—but if it was that same Booth (namely John Wilkes), he was acquainted with him.[11]

After his conversation with Farrell and Hardy, Mudd proceeded to return home. It was around 5:00 p.m. when he arrived back at the farm. On approaching his house, Mudd stated, the two strangers were already mounted on their horses getting ready to leave. "...I returned home leisurely, and found the two men were just in the act of leaving." Mr. Hensen (Herold) rode up to Dr. Mudd and inquired the shortest way to the house of a man named Parson Wilmer who lived near the Piney Church. Mr Tyser (Booth) was already some "...fifty to seventy yards" from where Mudd stood when Hensen (Herold) rode back to ask directions. According to Mudd's statement, he told Hensen (Herold) the most direct route to Wilmer's house after which Hensen (Herold) rode off, joining his partner in the direction of Mudd's short cut through the Zekiah Swamp. The route to Wilmer's is nearly due west of the Mudd house and directly opposite from Bryantown and the 13th New York Cavalry.

Sunday morning, April 16, Dr. Mudd attended church at St. Peter's where he met his "brother physician" and cousin, George Mudd.[12] Following church services, as George Mudd was on his way to the home of Henry Lowe Mudd, Sr. for Sunday dinner, he stopped to talk with his cousin Sam. According to George Mudd's testimony,[13] Samuel Mudd had told his cousin about the two suspicious persons who had been to his house the day before. George Mudd told the good doctor that the authorities should be notified. Samuel Mudd was reluctant to inform the soldiers in Bryantown of the strangers' visit, and asked George Mudd to do it for him.[14] George Mudd said that he would.

The next day, Monday, April 17, approximately forty hours after the two suspicious strangers left Samuel Mudd's farm, George Mudd rode

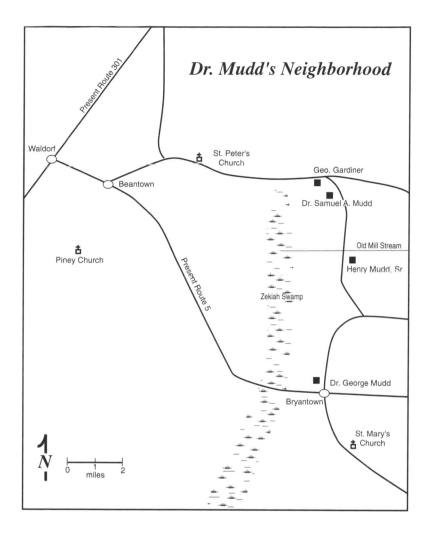

Dr. Mudd's Neighborhood

the short distance from his own farm to the Bryantown Tavern, and informed Lieutenant Dana of the 13th New York Volunteer Cavalry of his cousin's visitors.[15] George Mudd also informed Dana that one of the strangers had a broken leg and that his cousin had set it. Of course, no one had even suggested that the injured stranger was the assassin of the president, John Wilkes Booth, and so the government still had no knowledge or reason to believe that the fugitive was seriously crippled with a broken left leg. Such information would have been of vital importance to the government in their manhunt for Booth and Herold. But Samuel Mudd, now informed that the assassin of President Lincoln was the famous actor John Wilkes Booth, still contended that he did not know the two strangers other than by the names they gave him, Henson (Herold) and Tyser (Booth).

Home of Dr. Samuel A. Mudd

The road leading from the rear of the Mudd home. Booth and Herold presumably left along this route around five o'clock Saturday evening, April 15, 1865.

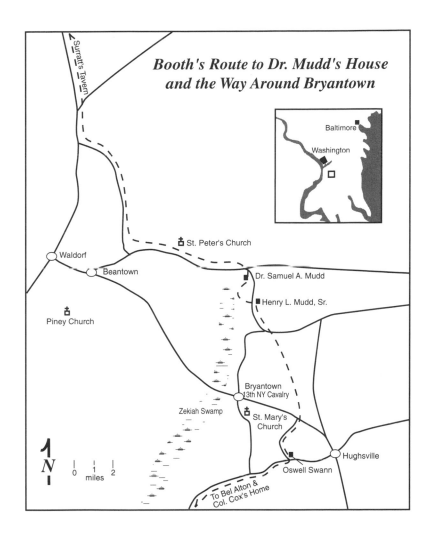

Booth's Route to Dr. Mudd's House and the Way Around Bryantown

As a result of George Mudd's information concerning his cousin, a team of detectives led by Lieutenant Alexander Lovett paid Dr. Mudd a visit on Tuesday morning, April 18, with the express purpose of interrogating the doctor about the two strangers.[16]

Mudd was questioned on Tuesday, April 18, and again on Friday, April 21, and according to Lieutenant Lovett's later testimony, again on Saturday, April 22.[17] From these interrogations two written statements were obtained from Mudd (see Appendices 1 and 2). The first statement is in Mudd's own hand and is undated (referred to as the "voluntary statement,") but presumably written down by Mudd sometime on Friday, April 21. The second statement was prepared by Colonel H. H. Wells after the Friday, April 21 interview (referred to as the "Wells statement"). This second statement was signed by Mudd and Wells on Saturday morning, April 22, when Mudd returned to Bryantown.

On Tuesday, April 18, Mudd was interrogated at his farm by Lieutenant Alexander Lovett and detectives William Williams, Joshua Lloyd and Simon Gavacan with George Mudd in tow. When the soldiers and George Mudd first arrived, Samuel Mudd was away from the house tending to work on the farm. Mrs. Mudd sent word to her husband to come, and while they waited for his return Lieutenant Lovett questioned Mrs. Mudd.

Mrs. Mudd told the soldiers what little she knew about the two strangers, stating that, "...one of them was a young man about eighteen or nineteen years of age. The other, who had a broken leg, was a man over thirty years."[18] She had left the room while the injured man was treated and the next time she saw him, "...she missed a moustache that he wore on his face when he entered the house." It was at this time that she also revealed a startling piece of information, almost casually, when she told the detectives that,

> ...her husband had furnished the man a razor for him to shave it off (his moustache) and when the man was leaving the house in the afternoon (Saturday approximately 4:00 p.m.) she took notice when he came to the foot of the stairs, that **his chin whisker became detached and that, she thought it was a false whisker.**[19]

When Mudd finally arrived at the farmhouse, there were more questions from Lovett. Mudd stated the essential facts as he claimed he remembered them. Two strangers came to see him; one had a broken leg caused by his horse falling on him which he treated. Mudd stated that **the two men were complete strangers to him, he had never seen them previously and did not know who they were**.

Mudd described the injured man as having a moustache and rather long chin whiskers. His companion was described by Mudd as, "a young man about seventeen or eighteen."[20] Mudd further stated that the injured man asked for a razor so that he might shave off his moustache which now, on reflection, Mudd thought suspicious. At the time of their leaving, Mudd claimed to have directed the two strangers to the road which would lead them across the Zekiah Swamp in the direction of Parson Wilmer's house at Piney Church. According to Lovett's later testimony, Mudd told the soldiers that he had heard of Lincoln's assassination while he was at church on Sunday morning, April 16.[21] Significantly, Mudd never mentioned the "false whisker" to the detectives, and equally significant, the detectives never asked Mudd about it waiting instead for him to volunteer it. He never did.

On Friday, April 21, the four detectives, along with several cavalrymen, returned to the Mudd farm to further their questioning of the doctor. The men had grown suspicious and, according to Lovett, came with the intention of arresting Mudd and taking him into custody. After interrogating Mudd at his farm, the soldiers took Mudd into custody to Bryantown where a formal statement was written down by Colonel Wells following Mudd's second questioning.

It was during this second interrogation at the Mudd house that Mudd made a startling revelation to the soldiers. Lieutenant Lovett had decided it was time to search the Mudd household, and on informing Mrs. Mudd of his intent, Dr. Mudd suddenly told his wife to go upstairs and bring down the boot which he had removed from the injured man's leg. Mrs. Mudd dutifully retrieved the boot and gave it to a surprised Lovett.

Carefully examining the boot, Lovett found the name *J. Wilkes* inscribed along the inner top edge. When Lovett called it to his attention, Mudd said, "he had not taken notice of that before."[22] Lovett now raised the issue of the false whiskers and Mudd finally "...said he was satisfied the stranger was Booth." Mudd did not, however, tell Lovett and the detectives at what precise moment he had deduced that the injured man at his house was John Wilkes Booth.

Following his questioning of Mudd that morning, Lovett took Mudd to Bryantown, and turned him over to Colonel H. H. Wells who was now in command of the troop of soldiers quartered there. After traveling a short distance along the main road to Bryantown, Mudd made another startling revelation. He told Lovett that he indeed knew John Wilkes Booth. He said that he had been introduced to Booth in November 1864 by a local man named John Thompson while attending Sunday services at St. Mary's Church in Bryantown. After this meeting, Mudd claimed that Booth had returned home with him and spent the night as his house guest. The following morning Mudd had taken Booth to his nearest neighbor, George Gardiner, where Booth bought a horse.[23] A horse characterized by having lost one eye.

Mudd was shown a photograph (carte de visite) of Booth, and was asked if the injured stranger resembled the man in the photo. Mudd thought that the photograph did not look like the injured stranger at first, but on reflection said it did resemble him "across the eyes." Although Mudd had maintained that the injured man kept a shawl wrapped around his face, and kept his face turned toward the wall so that his appearance was not obvious, he nevertheless gave a detailed description of the injured man which closely matched the features of Booth.

At some point, while he was in Bryantown being questioned further, Mudd wrote out a statement in his own hand summarizing what he had verbally told the officers.[24] In this voluntary statement, Mudd wrote, "I first heard of the assassination of President Lincoln on Saturday afternoon about two or three o'clock in the afternoon." At another point in his statement, Dr. Mudd said he heard of the assassination while in Bryantown. From his statement it is not clear who he heard it from, but it is clear from John Hardy's testimony that Mudd also heard, while in Bryantown, that John Wilkes Booth was the assassin.

St. Mary's Church near Bryantown, Maryland. John Wilkes Booth met with members of the Confederate underground at this church on at least two occasions in 1864. The first time was on Sunday, November 13, 1864; the second, on Sunday, December 18, 1864. It was during the first meeting that Booth was introduced to Dr. Mudd by Dr. William Queen's son-in-law, John Thompson, and it was after the second meeting in December that Booth stayed the night at Dr. Mudd's house, and purchased the one-eyed horse from George Gardiner the next day.

Also in his voluntary statement Mudd described his two visitors:

> ...one was a very small one. I should call him a well grown boy. He looked to be about 17 or 18—to be a boy who had never yet shaved. The other was a man of medium size, with black hair. He had whiskers, and also a moustache. ...The older...I should judge to be about 30 or 35 years of age.

Mudd also described the injured man as having a shawl wrapped around his head and shoulders partly concealing his face.[25] Upon their request, Mudd made a pair of crutches for the injured man, and was paid twenty-five dollars for his services. Mudd then related:

> No suspicion was aroused in my mind of anything being wrong with regard to these men. After I heard of the assassination and began to have suspicion as to these two men being in some way connected with it, a little circumstance occurred to me as confirmatory of such suspicions & which I had not thought of before. It was this. After breakfast the older one asked for a razor and some soap; which he got; and on my giving him the articles which I had prepared, a short time afterward, I noticed that his moustache had disappeared.[26]

Mudd concluded: "The injured man had a belt with two revolvers in it concealed under his clothing, which I discovered when he got into bed after having his wound dressed."[27]

The following morning, Saturday, April 22, Mudd returned to Bryantown for further questioning at the direction of Colonel Wells. It was at this time that Wells presented Mudd with a statement which Wells had prepared, and which Mudd was asked to read and sign.[28] While the second statement covers much of the same material in Mudd's earlier handwritten statement, it does contain certain new information. Mudd adds to his description of the injured man:

> He was a man, I should suppose about five feet ten inches high, and appeared to be pretty well made, but he had a heavy shawl on all the time. I suppose he would weigh 150 or 160 pounds. His hair was black and seemed to be somewhat inclined to curl; it was worn long. He had a pretty full forehead and his skin was fair. He was very pale when I saw him, and appeared as if accustomed to in-door rather than out-door life. ...I did not observe his hand to see whether it was small or large.[29] I have been shown the photograph of J. Wilkes Booth and I should not think that this was the man from any resemblance to the photograph, but from other causes I have every reason to believe that he is the man whose leg I dressed as above stated.[30]

Mudd, in this second statement, acknowledges for the first time that a prior meeting with Booth had occurred. "I have seen J. Wilkes Booth. I was introduced to him by Mr. J. C. Thompson, a son-in-law of Dr. William Queen, in November or December last."

The introduction was only a preamble, however. Mudd further states that Booth had actually stayed the night at his house.

> *The next evening he rode to my house and staid (sic) with me that night, and the next morning he purchased a rather old horse, but a very fine mover of Mr. George Gardiner, Sr., who resides but a short distance from my house.*

Then Mudd makes a very important statement. **"I have never seen Booth since that time to my knowledge until last Saturday night."** The statement is signed by Mudd, "Sam'l. A. Mudd," and by Wells, "Subscribed and sworn before me this 22nd day of April 1865 H. H. Wells Col. & P.M. Genl Def. S. of P."[31]

By now Lovett and Wells are certain that Mudd has been less than forthright in his several interviews with them. Lovett felt that Mudd was evasive in most of his answers, volunteering little. Each successive interrogation seemed to produce new and more valuable information on the identity and whereabouts of Booth and Herold. Convinced of Mudd's duplicity, Wells ordered the doctor taken into custody on Monday, April 24, and transported to Washington, D.C. where he was imprisoned in the old Capitol Prison (Carroll Annex) before being transferred to the eventual trial site at the old Washington Arsenal grounds (now Fort Lesley J. McNair.)

As Mudd arrived in Washington still uncertain of his fate, John Wilkes Booth arrived at the farmhouse of Richard Garrett near Port Royal, Virginia where he settled in after his trying and painful trip through southern Maryland.

5

THE MEETINGS.
NOT QUITE THE TRUTH, THE WHOLE TRUTH, AND
NOTHING BUT THE TRUTH.

When the government presented its case against Dr. Mudd, it had damaging evidence—evidence sufficient to convict Mudd. It did not, however, have all of the evidence against the good doctor.

What did the government know about Dr. Mudd when it went to trial? It knew that John Wilkes Booth and David Herold had come to Mudd's house early on Saturday morning, April 15, around 4:00 a.m., only five and a half hours after Booth shot Lincoln. It knew Mudd gave medical assistance to Booth by splinting his broken leg as well as feeding him and giving him a place to rest. It knew that Mudd was a former slaveholder and Southern sympathizer who opposed the Lincoln administration. And it knew, from Mudd's own admission, that he knew Booth from a meeting in November 1864.

The government also knew more. It knew of a second meeting between Booth and Mudd — a second meeting which involved John H. Surratt, Jr., and would prove damaging to Mudd's claim of innocence. What the government did not know, however, was that a third meeting had occurred involving Mudd and Booth, and a Confederate secret service agent.

While Dr. Mudd attempted to trivialize his admitted meeting with Booth in November 1864, the government knew better. The government had evidence that Mudd and Booth had actually met on two separate occasions in 1864, not one as originally claimed by Mudd. The second meeting took place in December 1864 in Washington, D.C. This second meeting was revealed by one of the government's star witnesses during his testimony at the trial.

At first, Mudd failed to inform the authorities of any of his meetings with Booth. It was only during his trip to Bryantown to meet with Colonel

Wells that Mudd acknowledged that he had met with Booth in November 1864. Mudd then said, "I have never seen Booth since that time to my knowledge until last Saturday night (April 15)."[1] The second meeting, which Mudd had withheld from Wells, took place in late December at Booth's hotel room in Washington, and would be introduced during the trial by the government's key witness, Louis J. Weichmann.[2] The third meeting would remain hidden until years later.

According to Mudd's statement to Wells, it was during the November visit that Booth stayed as an overnight guest in his house. Mudd also stated that it was during this November visit that he took Booth to his neighbor, George Gardiner, where Booth purchased the one-eyed horse subsequently used by Powell. Again Mudd lied. Booth did not stay the night during his November visit, nor did he purchase the one-eyed horse at that time. It was during a third meeting between Mudd and Booth that Booth stayed the night and purchased the one-eyed horse.

A memorandum prepared by the desk clerk of the National Hotel where Booth lodged when in Washington shows that Booth checked out of his hotel room on Friday, November 11.[3] He checked back into the hotel on Monday, November 14. Booth did go to Bryantown on the 11th where he spent the night at the home of Dr. William Queen, a member of the Confederate underground in Charles County.

On Sunday, November 13, Booth attended St. Mary's Church, a short distance southeast of Bryantown, where he was introduced to Samuel Mudd by Queen's son-in-law, John Thompson. Mudd acknowledges in his statement given to Wells that this meeting did occur. Contrary to Mudd's statement, however, Booth did not spend the night at Mudd's house, but returned to Washington as evidenced by the memorandum of the hotel desk clerk, and a letter written by Booth dated at Washington on November 14.[4] These two items clearly place Booth back in Washington on Monday, November 14.

If Booth did not stay at the Mudd house on the night of November 13, and did not purchase the one-eyed horse the next day as Mudd claimed, when did he? This suggests that Booth visited with Dr. Mudd in Charles County a second time—a third meeting not revealed by Mudd.

Booth did indeed visit Bryantown a second time. He was back at the Bryantown Tavern on the evening of December 17. As on his November trip, he was picked up by Dr. Queen, and stayed the first night at Queen's home. The following day, after church services at St. Mary's, Booth met with Dr. Mudd at the Bryantown Tavern where Mudd had arranged a meeting with Thomas Harbin, a Confederate Secret Service operative. Harbin was responsible for certain undercover operations in the lower Maryland counties that bordered the Potomac River.

Harbin was an extremely competent agent and could play a vital role assisting in the successful passage of Lincoln should Booth's plan of capture succeed. Harbin had been postmaster at Bryantown and was well

The meeting at the Bryantown Tavern on December 18, 1864.

The second meeting involving Mudd and Booth occurred in December immediately before the third meeting in Washington. It was at this meeting that Mudd introduced Booth to Thomas Harbin, a Confederate operative. As a result of this meeting, Harbin agreed to assist Booth in his capture conspiracy.

Edward Steers, Jr. collection
John Wilkes Booth

Courtesy of James O. Hall
Dr. Samuel A. Mudd

Courtesy of James O. Hall
Thomas Harbin

Courtesy of Surratt House and Museum

Bryantown Tavern ca. 1890.

acquainted with Dr. Mudd. Mudd introduced Booth to Harbin and after a "private conversation" between the three men, Harbin agreed to help Booth in his plan to carry the captured Lincoln to Richmond.[5]

Following their meeting at the tavern, Booth returned to Mudd's home where he spent the night on December 18. The following morning, Monday, December 19, Mudd and Booth visited George Gardiner where Booth purchased the one-eyed horse. Booth then returned to the Bryantown Tavern where George Gardiner's nephew, Thomas Gardiner, delivered the one-eyed horse to Booth the next day.[6]

The memorandum of National Hotel clerk Bunker places Booth at the National Hotel on Monday, November 14, and Tuesday, November 15. Clearly, Booth could not have been in two places at one time. This leads to the conclusion that it was during his second visit to Bryantown in mid-December that Booth visited with Mudd and purchased the one-eyed horse from Gardiner. This conclusion is supported by the testimony of Thomas Gardiner and John F. Hardy.

Booth received his newly-purchased horse from Thomas Gardiner on Tuesday, December 20, and subsequently rode him back to Washington. He arrived back in Washington at the National Hotel and checked in on Thursday, December 22.

Although missed by the government, and many researchers since,[7] other evidence exists which places Booth in Charles County in mid-December. During Thomas Gardiner's testimony relating to Booth's purchase of the horse, and Gardiner's delivery of it to Booth, Gardiner was asked whether he had ever heard of Booth being in the neighborhood before. Gardiner stated that he, "...did hear that he (Booth) was in the neighborhood of Bryantown some time before that." Clearly Thomas Gardiner places Booth in the area of Bryantown on two separate occasions, both times at St. Mary's, and one of those two times at the home of Samuel Mudd.

A second witness, John F. Hardy, a neighbor of Mudd, also testified to seeing Booth at St. Mary's Church near Bryantown on two separate occasions. The first time was in November, and the second was "...about a month after" but "...before Christmas." John F. Hardy gives the following testimony:

> Q. *The Booth that was spoken of was the one who had been there looking at lands. Is that what you asked?*
>
> A. *I saw a gentleman there that went by that name (Booth): I did not know who he was.*
>
> Q. *Where did you see him?*
>
> A. *I saw him some time before Christmas, at church, one Sunday.... Some time again I saw him at the same place, and asked if that was the same man; and the answer was, "Yes."*

Q. *When did you first see him?*

A. *Some time before Christmas: it may have been November. I will not be positive.*

Q. *Endeavor to refresh your recollection as to the dates of the two occasions that you saw Booth in the country.*

A. *I cannot call the dates: I do not remember any dates at all.*

Q. *How long were the two times apart?*

A. *I think about a month. It might not have been quite that length of time, and it may have been a little longer.*

Q. *The first time was about the 1st of November?*

A. *I think it was sometime in November.*

Q. *Early or late November?*

A. *That I cannot answer; but I think it must have been some time in November. I think both times that I saw him there were before Christmas; I am pretty sure it was, each time that I saw him there: and it strikes me it must have been in November when I first saw him there.*[8]

Hardy also testified to seeing Booth "...riding on the Horse Head Road, by himself" a day or two after seeing him at St. Mary's Church the second time:

Q. *Did you ever hear of his being in that part of the country, at any other except those two times, before the assassination?*

A. *No, sir: a day or two after the second time that I saw him at church, I met him a little above Bryantown, riding on the Horse Head Road, by himself; but I only call that about one time, as I think it was the next day after Sunday. On Monday evening, I rode to Bryantown to see if I could get my horse shod; and I met Mr. Booth, or the same man they called Booth,—I do not know who he was,—a little above Bryantown riding by himself. He was riding a horse in the road leading straight to Horse Head, or he could not come to this point, to Washington, on the same road.*[9]

Two eyewitnesses place Booth in the Bryantown area on two separate occasions: the first in November, and the second in December 1864. And it was on the second visit, according to Thomas Gardiner, that Gardiner delivered the horse to Booth at the Bryantown Tavern, not on the first visit.

But the most damaging evidence that places Booth in Charles County in December 1864 is from Mudd himself. This startling revelation appears in an affidavit by Mudd written in 1865 in response to a sworn statement by the officer in command of the military guard escorting Mudd to his imprisonment at Fort Jefferson.[10]

Following their convictions on July 7, 1865, Mudd, O'Laughlen, Arnold and Spangler were transported to Fort Jefferson in the Dry Tortugas where they were to begin serving their sentences. A military guard, commanded by Captain George W. Dutton (Company C, 10th Regiment, Veteran Reserve Corps) accompanied the prisoners to the fort. Following his return, Dutton filed an affidavit with Brigadier General Joseph Holt, the judge advocate general, on July 22, 1865 describing a conversation he had with Mudd. In his affidavit Dutton makes a damaging claim regarding Mudd. He states that while enroute to Fort Jefferson, Dr. Mudd "...confessed that **he knew Booth when he came to his house with Herold on the morning after the assassination of the President.**" And further, that Mudd "...also confessed that he was with Booth at the National Hotel on the evening referred to by Weichmann in his testimony; that he came to Washington on that occasion **to meet Booth by appointment;** who wished to be introduced to John Surratt;..." Neither of these two statements concerning Mudd were new to the government which suspected the first, and had proven the second.

Dutton's statement reached Mudd in prison which prompted Mudd to file an affidavit responding to Dutton's claims.[11] In his affidavit, dated August 28, 1865,[12] Mudd denies Dutton's claim that he confessed to knowing Booth, but did admit to the meeting at the National Hotel in which he introduced Booth to John Surratt. In his response, Mudd let slip a piece of information damaging to his case and supporting Booth's second visit to Bryantown in December. On describing his meeting with Booth, John Surratt and Louis Weichmann, which occurred in Booth's hotel room on December 23, 1864, Mudd writes:

> "We (Mudd and Booth) *started down one street, and then up another, and had not gone far when we met Surratt and Weichmann. Introductions took place, and we turned back in the direction of the hotel. ...After arriving in the room, I took the first opportunity presented to apologize to Surratt for having introduced him to Booth—a man I knew so little concerning. This conversation took place in the passage in front of the room (hallway) and was not over three minutes in duration. ...Surratt and myself returned and resumed our former seats (after taking drinks ordered) around a centre table, which stood midway the room and distant seven or eight feet from Booth and Weichmann. Booth remarked that he had been down to the country a few days before, and said that he had not yet recovered from the fatigue. Afterward he said he had been down in Charles County, and had made me an offer for the purchase of my land, which I confirmed by an affirmative answer; and he further remarked that on his way up (to Washington) he lost his way and rode several miles off the track.*

This is an extremely revealing statement by Mudd made only two months after he began serving his life sentence. While Mudd trivializes his meeting with Booth and his introduction of John Surratt to Booth, he reveals an even more damaging fact which emerges for the first time. Mudd quotes Booth as saying that he had been down in Charles County "...a few days before." This would be a few days before December 23. Booth was actually in Charles County from December 17 until December 22 when he returned to the National Hotel.[13] Mudd also reveals that he met with Booth at this time stating that Booth, "...had made me an offer for the purchase of my land, which I confirmed by an affirmative answer."[14]

Mudd is telling the truth for one of the few times in this whole episode. Booth had made another visit to Charles County just before December 23, and met with Mudd a second time at St. Mary's Church. It was during this second visit that the Confederate agent Thomas Harbin told of his meeting with Booth at the Bryantown Tavern which Harbin claimed was arranged by Mudd. At this important meeting, Harbin agreed to assist Booth in the safe passage of the captured Lincoln to Richmond.

Hardy's testimony places Booth on the Horse Head Road which would have placed Booth off of the main road back to Washington. Mudd writes in his statement, "... he (Booth) further remarked that on his way up he lost his way and rode several miles off the track." This would confirm John F. Hardy's testimony that he saw Booth riding along the Horse Head Road.

Booth finally returned to the National Hotel on Thursday, December 22 after this important meeting at the Bryantown Tavern where, with the helpful introduction by Mudd, he had enlisted the services of Thomas Harbin in his capture scheme. The following day, Friday, December 23, a third meeting between Booth and Mudd occurred, this time to enlist the services of John H. Surratt.

On the 23rd, Mudd and his cousin, Jeremiah T. Mudd, came to Washington from Charles County for the purpose of Christmas shopping, according to Jeremiah Mudd's testimony.[15]

While in Washington, Dr. Mudd and his cousin separated and Mudd went on to meet Booth on Pennsylvania Avenue near Booth's hotel. Booth had wanted Mudd to introduce him to John H. Surratt whose reputation as a Confederate courier had been made known to Booth.[16] Mudd had agreed to introduce Booth to Surratt and came to Washington to meet Booth for this purpose. This arrangement was presumably made while Booth stayed over at Mudd's house on Sunday, December 18.

Meeting in front of the National Hotel, Booth and Mudd started to walk up Seventh Street in the direction of the Surratt house located at 541 H Street a few blocks to the north. As Booth and Mudd walked up Seventh Street toward the boarding house they met John Surratt and Louis Weichmann coming down Seventh Street in the direction of Pennsylvania Avenue. The four men stopped and introductions were made, after which Booth invited the three men to join him in his hotel room a short distance from where they were standing.

The meeting at the National Hotel on December 23, 1864.

The third meeting involving Mudd and Booth took place in Booth's hotel room on December 23, 1864 during which Mudd introduced Booth to John H. Surratt, Jr. As a result of this meeting Surratt joined Booth's conspiracy to capture Lincoln.

Edward Steers, Jr. collection   Courtesy of James O. Hall   Courtesy of Surratt House and Museum

John Wilkes Booth   **Dr. Samuel A. Mudd**   **John H. Surratt**

Courtesy of James O. Hall

The National Hotel, Washington, D. C.

46

According to Louis J. Weichmann's testimony,[17] and Mudd's own affidavit, the four men returned to Booth's room where he ordered drinks and cigars for all. Weichmann's testimony details much of the actions of his three companions during this meeting which are also confirmed five years later by John Surratt in his famous Rockville Lecture.[18]

During the course of the meeting, Mudd and Booth stepped into the hall for private discussions and later were joined by Surratt. At some point, Mudd, Booth and Surratt sat around a table conversing, while Weichmann sat so that he could hear their conversation, but could not discern what was being discussed. Weichmann described how Booth took an envelope from his pocket and drew "lines" on it as if drawing a map. After approximately thirty minutes, the meeting adjourned, and Weichmann continued his visit with Mudd in the lobby of the Pennsylvania House hotel where Mudd was staying along with his cousin.[19]

Whatever actually transpired during the meeting in Booth's hotel room, one fact is sure: just as Thomas Harbin before him, John H. Surratt became a key member of Booth's conspiracy to capture the president as a result of his introduction to Booth by Dr. Mudd.

Mudd appears to be a principal recruiter for Booth, at least in regard to two very important members of his team: Thomas Harbin and John Surratt. Of all the conspirators enlisted into Booth's gang, Harbin and Surratt were the most competent and experienced, and the two who were already active agents of the Confederate underground.

When Dr. Mudd swore in his second statement dated April 22, 1865, that he had, "...never seen Booth since that time (November 1864 meeting) to my knowledge until last Saturday night," he deliberately lied. The three meetings which are described above were not casual or incidental meetings in which Mudd happened across Booth. In at least two of the meetings, Mudd was the arranger and the principal without whose participation the meetings could not be held. In these two meetings, Mudd introduced two key individuals into Booth's conspiracy group: Thomas Harbin and John H. Surratt.

Mudd steadfastly maintained that when Booth and Herold arrived at his house on Saturday, April 14, he acted only in the role of a good doctor who, when faced with a stranger in desperate need of medical assistance, did what his Hippocratic oath required him to do—render medical assistance. And, that upon finally becoming suspicious of his two late-night guests, he took the necessary steps to inform the military authorities of their visit. According to Mudd's story, when questioned by the military, he related all of the facts as he remembered them and withheld nothing from the authorities. For these innocent acts, the good doctor claimed, he was taken into custody and eventually charged as an accomplice in the murder of the president, and in aiding and abetting John Wilkes Booth's attempt to escape.

Mudd could not have been more disingenuous in his statements to the authorities nor in his later claims of innocence. At each turn he was attempting to cover his trail by volunteering information only when he was reasonably sure it would be found out anyway.

It would appear that Mudd did not want the authorities to find out about Booth's second visit to Charles County when Mudd arranged the critical meeting with Thomas Harbin. So he condensed the meetings in November and December into a single visit by Booth, at which time Booth stayed the night at Mudd's house and purchased the one-eyed horse. Mudd knew the authorities had found out about Booth's visit to Charles County in November and he hoped to conceal the second, more damning visit and it worked. The authorities, and for that matter many researchers, never realized that there was a second visit in December 1864.[20]

It is now clear that the scenario Mudd presented was a lie, and that he deliberately withheld the facts from the authorities. He revealed bits of information only when they became obvious to his interrogators, at the same time twisting the truth to cover his activities. Knowing the details of the three meetings involving Mudd and Booth, it is beyond reasonable belief to accept Mudd's claim that he had met Booth only by accident, and that he did not recognize him on the morning of April 15 when he sought medical assistance. Dr. Mudd's deliberate deceptions were the only way he could hope to avoid the gallows with his other accomplices.

6

WHAT DID MUDD KNOW
AND WHEN DID HE KNOW IT?

Lieutenant Lovett testified at the conspiracy trial that Mudd claimed to have first heard of Lincoln's assassination on Sunday, April 16, while at church.[1] Mudd attended St. Peter's Church on that Sunday and while there sought the counsel of his cousin, George Mudd, soliciting his help in reporting to the military authorities in Bryantown the visit of the two men to his house.

Lovett's testimony is at variance, however, with Mudd's own statement in which Mudd wrote, "I first heard of the assassination of President Lincoln on Saturday afternoon (April 15) about two or three o'clock in the afternoon."[2] Several paragraphs later in that same statement Mudd writes, "I first heard of the assassination of President Lincoln at Bryantown."

Mudd wrote that his purpose in going to Bryantown on Saturday, April 15, was to, "...purchase some articles which were needed by the family; and I thought I would at the same time see about some nails that were intended for immediate use. I purchased at Mr. Bean's some calico & some pepper, for which I paid him."[3] While Mudd acknowledges hearing of Lincoln's murder while in Bryantown, he does not tell us if he also heard who the assassin was. Did he not ask? Did the informant who told Mudd overlook telling him who the assassin was or did he simply not know? By Saturday afternoon the authorities had released the name of John Wilkes Booth as the assassin of Lincoln.

While claiming to be forthright and willing to tell all to his interrogators, Mudd is silent about this important point in each of his statements. His neighbors are not. That Mudd learned in Bryantown that the assassin was John Wilkes Booth comes from the testimony of two of his own friends.

Francis R. Farrell, a neighbor of Dr. Mudd's, lived midway between the Mudd house and Bryantown. Mudd acknowledges in his voluntary statement, and again in Colonel Wells' draft, visiting with John F. Hardy and Francis R. Farrell on his return trip from Bryantown Saturday afternoon. Farrell was called as a prosecution witness and under examination by Judge Advocate John A. Bingham, he stated that Mudd told him of Lincoln's assassination. Farrell states, "I asked the question who assassinated the President; and the doctor replied, and said, '**A man by the name of Booth.**'" Mr. Hardy then asked him if it was, "...the Booth that was down here last fall.[4] The doctor said that he did not know whether it was or not; ...if it was that one, he knew him."[5]

According to both Farrell and Hardy, Mudd knew that Booth was the assassin of Lincoln on Saturday afternoon while Booth was still at Mudd's home. Mudd's only defense at this point would be his claim to not have recognized Booth while Booth was at his house.

Mudd also withheld information about his identity as a mail courier along the Confederate mail line between Washington and Richmond. He further failed to reveal that he had gone to Bryantown on Saturday, not to purchase supplies, but to make a mail drop for the Confederate underground only to be confronted by Union soldiers.[6]

Several miles to the south of Bryantown was the home of a man named Thomas A. Jones. Jones, age 41, was a farmer who worked a stretch of land that fronted along the Potomac River. This land was situated along a high bluff which presented a clear view across the river of Confederate Virginia.[7] Jones served as one of the Confederate mail operatives and underground agents along the line from Richmond to Washington, and reported to Samuel Cox, his superior in the underground in Charles County.

Thomas Jones played a crucial role in the attempted escape of Booth and Herold during the first days of their flight. After leaving Mudd's home around 5:00 p.m. on Saturday evening, Booth and Herold made their way several miles south to the home of Colonel Samuel Cox near Bel Alton, Maryland.[8] Cox's home, known as Rich Hill, was situated a short distance from Thomas Jones' home.

The route Booth and Herold took to Cox's home was directly opposite the route that Mudd told the soldiers he had sent the two strangers on. Mudd testified that he sent the two strangers west, toward Parson Wilmer's at Piney Church. The route Booth and Herold actually took made a wide sweep to the east around Bryantown, as if Booth had known that a troop of Federal cavalry was making its headquarters there. The wide sweep to the east of Bryantown brought them into contact with a man named Oswell Swann, a black tobacco farmer whose cabin was located southeast of Mudd's farm. Swann agreed to escort the two fugitives across the Zekiah Swamp to the home of Colonel Cox.[9]

Arriving around 1:00 a.m. on Sunday morning, April 16, Booth and Herold spent the next several hours with Cox and his adopted 18 year old son, Samuel Cox, Jr. Shortly after breakfast on Easter Sunday morning,

Photograph by Edward Steers, Jr.

Thomas Jones' home known as "Huckleberry." Jones hid Booth and Herold in a pine thicket not far from his home, and safely sent the two fugitives over the Potomac River and into Virginia. Many years later Jones wrote a book which described his role in aiding Booth and Herold in their effort to escape.

Thomas A. Jones

Courtesy of James O. Hall

Jones was visited by Samuel Cox, Jr. who relayed the message that Colonel Cox wanted to see him right away. The two men rode over to the senior Cox's home, Rich Hill, where Cox informed Jones that the two fugitives were hiding in a thicket not two miles south. He told Jones to care for the men and to get them safely across the Potomac River to Virginia.

Jones, whose role as a Confederate agent also included ferrying persons back and forth across the river, was well suited for such a task. According to Jones himself, he never questioned the Colonel's directive, but set about his task like a good soldier. In 1893, twenty-eight years after the events associated with his efforts, Jones wrote a book in which he detailed much of what he knew.[10]

Since the military was extremely active throughout the area in the first hours following the assassination, Jones felt that an attempt to cross the river immediately was too risky. He found the two fugitives hiding in a small pine thicket not far from the Cox plantation, and told them to stay low until the right moment arrived when he could put them into the river.[11]

Jones' help was vital to the survival of Booth and Herold. It was Jones who literally sustained the two men for five days by providing both provisions and newspapers from Sunday, April 16, through Thursday, April 20. Without Jones' capable help and careful monitoring of the military activities in the area, Booth and Herold would surely have been captured or killed in the effort.[12]

Rich Hill, the home of Samuel Cox.

Late Thursday evening, April 20, Jones came for the two men. After leading them to the edge of the river, he placed them in a boat and pushed them into the river and toward the Virginia shore. Booth and Herold did not make it to Virginia that night, but wound up back on the Maryland shore at the farm of John J. Hughes along Nanjemoy Creek, some distance to the north of where they were first launched by Jones. After hiding all day Friday and Saturday, April 21 and 22, Booth and Herold made a second attempt to cross the river which proved successful. They landed on the Virginia side early Sunday morning.

Later on the morning of April 23, Booth and Herold were placed in the capable hands of Thomas Harbin, the Confederate agent introduced to Booth by Mudd at the Bryantown Tavern only four months before.[13] The meeting between Booth and Harbin which Mudd had arranged in December now proved a godsend to Booth. Harbin made the necessary arrangements to see the two men safely to their next stop along the escape route.

Jones' efforts were heroic to the successful escape of Booth and Herold across the river into Confederate Virginia. Although arrested and thrown into old Capital Prison in the general roundup through St. Mary's County,

Courtesy James O. Hall

Colonel Samuel Cox

Courtesy James O. Hall

Samuel Cox, Jr.

Booth visited Cox after he left Mudd's house on Saturday evening. Years later, Samuel Cox, Jr. would write of Mudd's revelations concerning Booth and his visit on Saturday, April 15, 1865.

the authorities never knew of Jones' role in harboring and successfully aiding Booth and Herold in their escape.

Years later, Jones wrote the details of the events surrounding his summons by Colonel Cox to Rich Hill, and of hiding Booth and Herold in a pine thicket until successfully placing them on the Potomac. Subsequent to its publication in 1893, a copy of Jones' book was owned by Samuel Cox, Jr., and passed through his descendants where it was eventually examined by the Lincoln assassination researcher, James O. Hall.[14] Of particular interest in this privately held volume is a series of annotations made in various key parts of the book by Samuel Cox, Jr.

In 1877, according to Samuel Cox, Jr., after Dr. Mudd's release from prison, he and Dr. Mudd were candidates for the Maryland state legislature. The two men canvassed Charles County together during this period and, according to Cox, privately discussed the events of 1865 concerning John Wilkes Booth and Davy Herold.

Cox writes in his annotations that Mudd confided to him that shortly after setting Booth's leg Mudd had taken,

> ...letters he had but a short time had gotten through the contraband mail for distribution, and that in going to Bryantown to mail them[15] he was surprised to find the village surrounded by soldiers and upon being stopped by a sentry, ...he was horrified when told the president had been shot the night before, and, upon asking who had shot him **the fellow had answered Booth**.

These revelations are significant in themselves, but Cox relates even more damaging statements about Mudd:

> He (Mudd) then told me his first impulse was to surrender Booth, that he had imposed upon him, had twice forced himself upon him and now a third time, had come with a lie upon his tongue and received medical assistance which would be certain to have him serious trouble but he determined to go back and upbraid him for his treachery which he did. And that Booth had appealed to him in the name of his Mother whom he professed to love so devotedly and that he acted and spoke so tragically that he told them they must leave his house which they did and after getting in with Oswald Swann they were piloted to Rich Hill. Aug 7 1893 S Cox Jr.

Cox supports the claim that Mudd was not only thoroughly acquainted with Booth, but knew that it was Booth at the time he gave him medical assistance.[16] According to Cox's annotations, Mudd acknowledged that Booth had visited with him on two occasions in Charles County when he stated that Booth, "...had twice forced himself upon him...." Cox also reveals Mudd's confession to be a mail agent for the Confederacy going to Bryantown to mail Confederate letters he had recently received for distribution.

There is still further corroboration of Mudd's knowledge that his patient was the assassin Booth. Following Mudd's conviction and sentencing, he, along with Arnold, O'Laughlen and Spangler, was transported under military guard to Fort Jefferson in the Dry Tortugas off the coast of Florida. Commanding the guard that escorted Mudd and his fellow prisoners was a young officer, Captain George W. Dutton, Co. C, 10th Veteran Reserve Corps. Following his escort duty, Dutton, in a sworn affidavit, stated that Dr. Mudd,

> ...confessed that he knew Booth when he (Booth) came to his house with Herold on the morning after the assassination of the President; that he had known Booth for some time, but was afraid to tell of Booth's having been at his house on April 15, fearing that his own and the lives of his family would be endangered thereby.[17]

Dutton's affidavit corroborates the statements made by Samuel Cox, Jr. Neither Cox nor Dutton were associated in any way and there is no known evidence suggesting that they ever met or even communicated with one another at any time. Most importantly, Cox's annotations were not made until 1893, twenty-eight years after Dutton filed his affidavit with the judge advocate. Just as Cox's claims, Dutton's statement rings true. There would be no purpose to fabricating such a statement at the time since Mudd had already been charged, tried and sentenced, and was enroute to the prison where he was about to begin serving his sentence. Nothing was gained by Dutton, the judge advocate or the government by fabricating such a story post facto.

The statements made by Samuel Cox, Jr. and George Dutton make Mudd's claim that Booth wore a disguise, and that Mudd failed to recognize Booth, nonsense. To believe Cox and Dutton is further evidence that Mudd lied about what he knew and when he knew it. Upon learning of Dutton's affidavit, Mudd filed his own in response to it.[18]

In addition to the statements already discussed, there exists one other revealing document which is damaging to Dr. Mudd's case. When George Atzerodt walked into the bar of the Kirkwood Hotel around 10:00 p.m. on the night of the assassination, he was only moments away from carrying out the task Booth had assigned to him of assassinating Vice President Andrew Johnson.

Fortunately, Atzerodt's courage evaporated and he fled the hotel, mounted his horse and rode away in the direction of Ford's Theatre. Seeing the great commotion along Tenth Street in front of the theater, the frightened Atzerodt returned his horse to a stable on Eighth Street, and began wandering about the city, half drunk and half in terror. He boarded a horse-drawn trolley at Seventh Street and Pennsylvania Avenue, and made a round trip to the Navy Yard before returning to his old haunt, the Kimmel House (also referred to as the Pennsylvania House), where he flopped for the night.[19]

Early Saturday morning Atzerodt arose and walked to Georgetown where he boarded a stage for Rockville, Maryland, located to the northwest of the city. Atzerodt eventually made his way to Germantown, Maryland, some twenty-five miles northwest of Washington. He went to the house of his cousin, Hartman Richter, and safely settled down with his relatives, or so he thought.[20]

On Thursday, April 20, Atzerodt was taken into custody by a troop of Union soldiers and transported to Washington where he was eventually imprisoned at the Washington Arsenal along with other conspirators who had been arrested earlier. On May 1, 1865, between the hours of 8:00 p.m. and 10:00 p.m, Atzerodt was visited by his brother-in-law, John L. Smith, and the provost marshall of Baltimore, James L. McPhail.[21]

Smith, an assistant to McPhail, had gotten word of Atzerodt's arrest. He convinced McPhail to accompany him to Washington to seek permission to visit his brother-in-law and find out what sort of trouble he had gotten himself into.

McPhail and Smith were granted permission to visit the prisoner and interview him. During a two hour interview McPhail transcribed a lengthy statement from Atzerodt which failed to reach the authorities. Instead, McPhail apparently turned the statement over to Captain William E. Doster, former provost marshall of the District of Columbia, who had been appointed by the War Department as defense counsel for Atzerodt. Doster put the statement safely away among his personal papers where it remained until its rediscovery in 1978.[22]

In Atzerodt's statement describing his own role as a member of Booth's plot to capture Lincoln, Atzerodt confirms Thomas Harbin's role: "Thos. Holborn (Harbin) was to meet us on the road and help in the kidnapping." While Atzerodt reveals certain details of the conspiracy, he also mentions several individuals who were involved to varying degrees. In a surprising revelation, Atzerodt tells McPhail, "I am certain **Dr. Mudd knew all about it, as Booth sent liquors & provisions for the trip with the president to Richmond, about two weeks before the murder to Dr. Mudd's.**"

According to Atzerodt's statement, Booth entrusted Mudd with storing these supplies. Booth and his cohorts could then provision themselves after capturing Lincoln. That provisions were sent to Mudd's two weeks before the actual assassination suggests that Booth's decision to murder Lincoln occurred sometime between then and April 12.

Dr. Mudd's name surfaces yet again in connection with Booth's escape to Virginia. After Booth and Herold safely reached the Virginia shore Sunday morning, April 23, Herold made his way to the home of Mrs. Elizabeth Quesenberry, a Confederate agent who was well connected to Thomas Harbin. Harbin maintained a signal camp not far from the Quesenberry home. Leaving the injured Booth with their small boat,[23] Herold made his way to the Quesenberry home where he negotiated with the Confederate lady. Hearing Herold out, Mrs. Quesenberry knew who to send for. Within the hour, Thomas Harbin arrived and took charge of the two fugitives. Harbin passed Booth and Herold over to one of his operatives, a man named William Bryant, with instructions for Bryant[24] to get the men to the home of a wealthy planter by the name of Dr. Richard Stuart.[25]

Stuart had been engaged in drug smuggling for the Confederacy, and had even spent time in jail under suspicion of being a Confederate operative, but never for very long. While his precise role with the Confederate underground is clouded, he was a well-trusted Confederate operative in his own right in King George County, Virginia.

Mudd's introduction of Harbin to Booth in December at the Bryantown Tavern would now serve Lincoln's assassin well, emphasizing again the crucial role that Mudd played in Booth's operation to capture Lincoln. Without Harbin, Booth and Herold would have been stranded on the Virginia side of the river. Bryant, following Harbin's instructions, provided horses for the two men, and took them to the home of Dr. Stuart. It was around dinner time on Sunday evening when Bryant arrived with his two weary fugitives.

Booth and Herold were not well received by Stuart, who by now knew of Lincoln's murder and knew who Booth and Herold were. It was a "no win" situation for Stuart who, now that the war was over in Virginia, did not need to become involved in any way with Lincoln's assassination.

Although Stuart refused lodging and medical help to Booth, he did provide the two fugitives with food and allowed them to refresh themselves. After feeding the two, Stuart insisted that Bryant get them off of his property. He told Bryant to take them to the cabin of a free black named William Lucas, which adjoined Stuart's property.[26]

Two weeks after Booth's capture at the Garrett farm, Stuart was taken into custody[27] at which time he gave his interrogators a statement concerning the fugitives' visit on Sunday night.[28] In his statement Stuart said that one of the men had said to him that he had been recommended to the men by Dr. Mudd: "... they said Dr. Mudd had recommended them to me."[29] Stuart denied knowing Dr. Mudd personally, but acknowledged he knew of "...Mudds in Maryland." If Stuart is to be believed, Dr. Mudd knew where Booth and Herold were heading when they rode away from his property on Saturday evening, and that Stuart, a Confederate sympathizer and a fellow physician, was a required stop once the two reached Virginia. Importantly, Dr. Stuart's home was not on the way to Washington where Mudd had claimed the two men were headed when they left his house.

Richard Stuart's statement is further corroborated by the statement of William Bryant. Bryant had guided the fugitives from Quesenberry's house to Stuart's. In a deposition given by Bryant following his arrest on May 6,

Cleydale, the summer home of Dr. Richard Stuart located in King George County, Virginia. Booth and Herold arrived at Cleydale Sunday evening, April 23, 1865. According to a later statement by Dr. Stuart, Herold had told Stuart that they were referred to him by Dr. Mudd.

Cedar Grove, the home of Dr. Richard Stuart located on the Potomac River.

Bryant quoted David Herold as telling him, "I was recommended to Dr. Stuart to have something done to my brother's leg." Bryant elaborated further, "In going along I asked him what made him want to go to Dr. Stuart's; I mentioned other doctors who were more convenient. He said the reason was because he was recommended to Dr. Stuart."[30]

Of the handful of people who could have made such a recommendation, only Dr. Mudd is mentioned by name, and then by Richard Stuart himself. The government had both depositions in hand when it brought its charges against Mudd, and had no doubt that the doctor lied when he said he sent the two strangers off in the direction of Parson Wilmer's near Piney Church.

7

THE CASE AGAINST DR. MUDD

The case against Dr. Mudd[1] may be found in the government's specification which reads in part:

> ...the said Samuel A. Mudd did, ...advise, encourage, receive, entertain, harbor and conceal, aid and assist, the said John Wilkes Booth, ...with knowledge of the murderous and traitorous conspiracy aforesaid, and with intent to aid, abet, and assist ...in the execution thereof, and in escaping justice after the murder of the said Abraham Lincoln...[2]

The accusations against Mudd can be summarized as: 1) participating in the plot to assassinate Lincoln, and 2) knowingly aiding and abetting the escape of Lincoln's murderer. Certainly Dr. Mudd did not know of, or participate in, any plot to murder the president. The government, however, did not distinguish between the original conspiracy to capture Lincoln, and the ultimate conspiracy which resulted in his murder, and neither did the law. The murder of the president was an extension of the conspiracy to capture. Jefferson Davis had clearly understood that. In 1862, he had been correct when he concluded that any attempt to capture the president of the United States would surely result in killing, thus converting the plan of capture to one resulting in murder. The case against Mudd as a knowing accomplice in aiding Booth and Herold in their escape effort is substantial and compelling.

The appropriate venue for trying the accused, whether before a military tribunal or before a civil court, is a separate question from Dr. Mudd's guilt as an accomplice. It has no bearing on our consideration of the historical evidence in determining the guilt or innocence of Dr. Mudd. Too often, students of Dr. Mudd's case equate their belief that the military tribunal was the wrong court with Mudd's alleged innocence. The conclusion is frequently drawn that if it can be established that the tribunal was without legal jurisdiction, Mudd must be innocent. Mudd's guilt or innocence, and the jurisdiction of the tribunal are two separate questions and should not be confused.

On the one hand, the military tribunal may have lacked legal jurisdiction, but the accused could have been guilty. On the other hand, the military tribunal may have had legal jurisdiction, and the accused could have been innocent. The primary concern then, must be with the guilt or innocence of Dr. Mudd based on the evidence at hand, and not the jurisdiction of the military tribunal or whether he should have been tried in a civilian court.

In considering the case against Dr. Mudd, key questions center around whether Dr. Mudd had knowledge of a conspiracy to act against the president, knowledge which he withheld from the appropriate authorities, and which ultimately resulted in Lincoln's murder.

Was Dr. Mudd, in fact, a participant in the conspiracy to act against the president, from which he could withdraw prior to its commission only by reporting it to the authorities; and, did he knowingly aid and abet the assassins of the president after the act? These questions are linked, and fall heavily on the side of Mudd's guilt.

In judging Mudd's role in the conspiracy to capture the president, a conspiracy which led to his murder, consider the following facts of evidence:

Mudd's knowledge of, and acquaintance with, John Wilkes Booth.
1. The meeting in November 1864, in which Booth is first introduced to Mudd at St. Mary's Church in Bryantown.
2. The meeting at the Bryantown Tavern in mid-December 1864, (December 17-21) where Dr. Mudd introduced Booth to Thomas Harbin, and when Booth spent the night at Mudd's house and later purchased the one-eyed horse from his neighbor, George Gardiner.
3. The December 23, 1864 trip to Washington where Mudd meets Booth at the National Hotel and introduces him to Confederate agent John H. Surratt, Jr.

Whether Mudd knew that Booth murdered Lincoln, and when he knew it.
1. Samuel Mudd's statement that he had heard of the assassination while in Bryantown on Saturday afternoon (April 15).
2. Francis R. Farrell's testimony in which he states that Mudd told both himself, and John F. Hardy on Saturday afternoon that a man named Booth had murdered Lincoln.
3. Samuel Cox, Jr.'s statement that Mudd told him, in 1877, that while in Bryantown on Saturday afternoon, April 15, Mudd had heard of the assassination of President Lincoln, and that John Wilkes Booth was the assassin.

4. Samuel Cox, Jr.'s statement that Mudd told him that when he learned Booth was the assassin he returned home and ordered Booth out of his house.
5. Captain George W. Dutton's affidavit that Mudd told him on July 22, 1865, that he knew it was Booth whose leg he had set at his home on Saturday, April 15.

Evidence linking Mudd to Booth's conspiracy to capture President Lincoln.
1. Mudd's introduction of Thomas Harbin to Booth.
2. Mudd's introduction of John H. Surratt, Jr. to Booth.
3. Samuel Cox, Jr.'s statement which quotes Mudd as saying that he went into Bryantown on Saturday, April 15, to mail contraband letters which he had received earlier.
4. George Atzerodt's "lost confession" in which Atzerodt states that Booth had sent provisions to Dr. Mudd's house to be used for their flight to Virginia.
5. Dr. Richard Stuart's deposition which states that Herold had told him that Dr. Mudd had referred Booth and Herold to Dr. Stuart, implying that Booth would receive medical assistance.
6. William Bryant's statement that the two fugitives were referred to Dr. Stuart for medical assistance.

In the language of the law—would a reasonable person believe that Mudd was well acquainted with John Wilkes Booth? Would a reasonable person believe that Mudd had knowledge of Booth's conspiracy to capture Abraham Lincoln, and knowingly aided that conspiracy? Would a reasonable person believe that Mudd recognized John Wilkes Booth as the patient he gave medical treatment to early on the morning of April 15, 1865?

The three meetings involving Booth and Mudd which resulted in introducing John Surratt and Thomas Harbin into Booth's conspiracy, together with the statement by George Atzerodt that Booth had sent provisions to Mudd's to be used during the escape, clearly identifies Mudd as a willing conspirator in Booth's original plot.

Mudd's knowledge of the assassination, and that the assassin was John Wilkes Booth is evident from Mudd's own statements and the statements of Francis Farrell and John Hardy.

Mudd's knowledge that the injured man resting at his house on Saturday, April 15, was John Wilkes Booth is attested to by George Dutton and Samuel Cox, Jr., and from the evidence that Mudd and Booth had met on at least three prior occasions, and conducted business which furthered Booth's plot.

The evidence clearly shows that Mudd had knowledge of and participated in Booth's conspiracy to capture Lincoln. And following Lincoln's murder, he knowingly aided and abetted Booth in his escape.

There can be little doubt that Mudd recognized Booth when Booth came to his home early Saturday morning following the murder of Lincoln. Whether Booth had told Mudd that he had just murdered Lincoln is arguable. But what is not arguable is the fact that Mudd soon learned that Lincoln had been murdered, and that Booth was the murderer.

Knowing that his patient was the man accused of murdering the president, Mudd waited until Sunday morning church services to inform his cousin of the two visitors, and then asked his cousin to notify the authorities rather than inform them himself. George Mudd did not inform the authorities in Bryantown until Monday, April 17, more than forty hours after the two fugitives left Mudd's house. This delay proved crucial to Booth and Herold, allowing them ample time to reach Samuel Cox's plantation where they received much-needed help.

It was Dr. Mudd's contention then, and it is the contention of his defenders now, that Mudd did not know that the injured man he treated was John Wilkes Booth. This is based primarily on the claim made by Mudd that Booth wore a false beard while at Mudd's house, and effectively hid his features behind a shawl which he kept closely wrapped about his head and face.

A careful reading of the two statements given by Mudd shows that he gave an accurate description of Booth. Mudd's claim that Booth wore false whiskers to hide his identity is beyond belief when the evidence is carefully reviewed. Booth made no effort to hide his identity prior to arriving at Mudd's house, or after leaving the Mudd house. There is no evidence to show that Booth tried to hide his identity from any of the other people he came into contact with during his escape. Why would he choose to single out Mudd and attempt to disguise himself only in Mudd's presence?

Booth was well acquainted with Mudd as evidenced from their prior meetings. What purpose would be served by Booth hiding his identity from Mudd by wearing a disguise? The story of a false beard can only be found in Mudd's one statement of April 21, and nowhere else in the numerous encounters Booth had during his subsequent escape.

If Mudd truly did not know that his visitor was John Wilkes Booth, then when he subsequently found out in Bryantown that Lincoln had been murdered by Booth, it would have little consequence for the doctor other than being "horrifying news." But if Dr. Mudd knew that the injured man resting in his home was John Wilkes Booth, his obligation under the law was clear and unequivocal. Dr. Mudd was required to inform the authorities that the alleged murderer of the president was at his home. Mudd's only concern would be for the personal safety of his wife and children who were at that moment with Booth and Herold at the doctor's farm. The government believed that Mudd knew his injured patient to be Booth, and rightly concluded that Mudd knowingly aided and abetted his escape.

But the evidence suggests more than aiding and abetting. It strongly suggests that Dr. Mudd was a knowing and active participant in Booth's conspiracy to capture Lincoln, a conspiracy that resulted in murder. The evidence shows that Dr. Mudd met with Booth on at least three occasions. On two of these occasions he introduced Booth to two key individuals who became active participants in his conspiracy. These individuals were well known Confederate operatives, and they played key roles in Booth's plans. Further evidence suggests that Booth sent provisions to Mudd's house to be used by the escape party.

At the time of Mudd's first meeting with Booth at St. Mary's Church in November 1864, Booth was a well known leading actor with a national reputation. His family was considered the first family of the American stage. Booth's father, who died in 1852, had been the leading Shakespearean actor in England and later in America. Booth's older brother Edwin succeeded his father in that role. John Wilkes Booth's acting career was only a step behind his more famous brother. But whereas Edwin supported the Union, John's politics swung in the opposite direction. His views were well known and thought by most who described them as being in the extreme. A reasonable person would have no problem believing that Dr. Mudd knew of Booth well before they ever met, and had quickly become familiar with him after they met.

The fact that both Dr. Mudd and John Wilkes Booth shared a common passion for the Confederacy and desired its success was not incidental. Mudd, a former slaveholder, was more than just pro-Confederate; he felt that to lose the Confederacy would be to lose his special way of life.

Mudd was strongly opposed to black suffrage, and believed that blacks were beneath his dignity. In several letters which Mudd wrote while in prison to family members back home, he revealed his negative attitudes concerning blacks.

Within a few months of Mudd's imprisonment, on September 25, 1865, he attempted to escape from Fort Jefferson aboard the supply ship, *Thomas A. Scott.* The attempt failed when Mudd was discovered hiding beneath a plank in the ship's hold and he was returned to the prison. Mudd's defenders explain the escape attempt by saying that Mudd only wanted to reach Key West where he could obtain a writ of habeas corpus and hopefully secure his freedom.[3] Mudd himself refuted this claim by his apologists, and gave a different explanation for his attempted escape. On October 18, 1865 in a letter to his wife he wrote:

> ...it is bad enough to be a prisoner in the hands of white men, your equals under the Constitution, but to be lorded over by a set of ignorant, prejudiced and irresponsible beings of the unbleached humanity, was more than I could submit to....[4]

Three days later, in a letter dated October 21, 1865, to his brother-in-law, Mudd reveals the real reason for attempting to escape:

> *No man can say naught against the Conduct of either of us up to the present, other than my individual effort to get away, and I plead my apprehensions...the humiliation of being guarded by an ignorant, irresponsible & prejudiced negro Soldiery, before an Enlightened People as a justification. We are now guarded entirely by negro soldiers & a few white Officers a skins difference. ...Could we have had the White Regiment, the 161st N.Y.V. to guard the place no thought of leaving should have been harbored for a moment.*[5]

Being placed under a negro guard was more than Mudd could bear, and forced his escape attempt. Mudd also writes to his wife, telling her his feelings about returning to a community in which blacks have become the majority:

> *I am sorry to hear of the death of George Garrico and Mr. Bean. Our white population is wonderfully diminishing by death and other causes. The negroes will soon be in the majority, if not already. Should I be released anytime shortly, and circumstances permit, I will use all my endeavors to find a more congenial locality.*[6]

Dr. Mudd's own writings show that he was anti-black, a view ardently shared by John Wilkes Booth. It is also clear that Mudd was sympathetic to Booth, and shared his political views completely.

It is not unreasonable to think that Mudd desired the Confederacy's success in separating from the Union. He was not alone in this view. That Dr. Mudd would have participated in some way to help bring about a successful separation between the Northern and Southern states is both reasonable and understandable.

Despite his statement in which he claimed to be a "Union man," Mudd's sympathies were clearly anti-Union.[7] Mudd lied to his interrogators when he claimed support for the Union. If Mudd was a Union man, as he claimed in his statement to Wells, it was only under a perverse Union that still believed in slavery and the inferiority "...of ignorant, prejudiced and irresponsible beings of the unbleached humanity...." With Mudd, as with so many others, it was Union our way or no way at all.

As with his position regarding blacks, Mudd has left a written record explaining his views on Northern society and Abraham Lincoln. In 1862, Mudd wrote a letter to Orestes A. Brownson, a Catholic scholar and publisher of a leading Catholic journal of the period entitled *Brownson's Quarterly Review*. In his letter, Mudd explains what he means by Union:[8]

*The South even those termed Seceders and Leaders of Secession—
desire Union! Yes Union!*

*The people of the South are differently constituted from those of the
North—attributable to education and climate. ... they are more sensi-
tive—their sense of honor is much more keen and they would sooner run
the risk of death, than live with an injured reputation.*

And further:

*The people of the North are Puritanical, long faced or Methodistic and
hypocritical—they deal in Sympathetic language to hide their deception—
their actions are Pharisaical, covert, stealthy, and cowardly. They are law
abiding so long as it bears them out in their selfish interest, and praisers
and scatterers and followers of the Bible so long as it does not conflict with
their passions. They make good cow drivers, pickpockets and gamblers.*

*...Your people have so degenerated, that were it not for the foreign
element—which you possess—there would be only war on parchment, as
it is, there is just enough of true Yankee to make the rest good for nothing,
but an expense to the Nation.*

And finally, Mudd reveals his feelings about Lincoln and his Republican cohorts:

*...I regret sincerely to see such a lack of Patriotism in the Present
Administration and in the representatives of the North. They are dreamy
and mystified—they rush headlong regardless of law and its consequences
and skulk like sheep-stealing dogs, when another nation stands up in open
contravention. I confidently assert that if there was any other man
at the head of the Government of true conservative and constitutional principals, the Revolution would immediately cease so far
as the South is concerned.*

Was Mudd suggesting the removal of Lincoln? Mudd's vitriolic attack
on Brownson, and on Northerners in general, as well as his statements
regarding his black guards belies the humanitarian mantle he professed to
wear. Consider Mudd's pointed condemnation of Northerners as, "...law
abiding so long as it bears them out in their selfish interest...." One wonders how Mudd would have characterized his own behavior when dealing
with his lawful interrogators three years later. Mudd's letter to Brownson
would have surely helped to place a noose around Mudd's neck had it been
known at the time of his trial and subsequent sentencing.

Dr. Mudd's contribution to the capture conspiracy was not restricted to
arranging the introduction of Thomas Harbin and John Surratt to the plan.
Atzerodt's statement of May 1 that provisions were sent to Dr. Mudd's
farm by Booth to aid in the escape along the Confederate line is further
damage to Mudd's defense. Since Booth's original escape route did not

pass by Mudd's farm, it can be surmised that the provisions which Booth had sent were to be shipped to some other point along this original escape route.

The most damaging evidence against Dr. Mudd's case is that which supports the charge that he knew John Wilkes Booth at the time of his visit seeking medical care; that he subsequently learned that Booth had murdered Lincoln, and that he failed to turn Booth over to the authorities. Knowing that troops were in Bryantown, Mudd further aided Booth by sending him off in the direction of Samuel Cox and even recommending Dr. Richard Stuart to him.

Why would Mudd do such a thing? Evidence does support the view that when Booth arrived at Mudd's house in the early morning hours of April 15, Mudd knew nothing of Lincoln's assassination. The evidence also supports the view that Mudd would have no role in any plan to murder the President, albeit more from faintheartedness than a humanitarian concern. Why then would Mudd have jeopardized himself? The explanation is obvious. Mudd had become an active participant when he aided Booth's plan to capture Lincoln. Perhaps his participation was only around the edges at first, but eventually Mudd was sitting close to the center. Aiding and abetting Booth in the capture plan was one thing; murder was another. But once Mudd became embroiled in Booth's plan, there was no way out. Booth could and would implicate Mudd to the authorities with disastrous results. Mudd knew this.

When Mudd arrived in Bryantown the afternoon of April 15 and found out what Booth had done, he probably experienced panic, and then outrage. As he stood facing the military authorities in Bryantown, Mudd could have easily given Booth up, and ended it cleanly—except for one thing. Mudd knew that he was already deeply involved with Booth and his plans and that there was a trail which tied him close enough to Booth to hang him. Mudd had to do his best to cover that trail or point it in a different direction—away from himself.

Mudd was between a rock and a hard place. To give up Booth, Booth would have surely given up Mudd.[9] Mudd was in no position to tell the soldiers where Booth was unless he was sure that Booth would die in the attempt to capture him, and that was too uncertain. Mudd also had to consider his wife and children. They were with Booth at the very moment Mudd was in Bryantown. Mudd had to think it was possible that Booth would use them to his advantage in his effort to flee. Booth would not have given himself up without a fight, as evidenced by his final hours.

Mudd's only chance was for Booth to get out of his house, off of his farm, and as far away as possible, perhaps Mexico, Cuba or Europe. Mudd did the only thing he could do. He returned home, and as Samuel Cox, Jr. later wrote, upbraided Booth for his treachery and told him to get out fast.[10]

In doing this, Mudd surely told Booth that Bryantown was a hornet's nest, filled with angry soldiers who were looking everywhere for him, and that he had better skirt around Bryantown to the east and make his way to William Burtles' place or to Samuel Cox's home before attempting to cross the Potomac.[11]

Mudd's story that Booth and Herold wanted to go to Parson Wilmer's (also a good Union man) was a ruse. To have done so would have endangered them substantially more than swinging east where they eventually met Oswell (Oswald) Swann who successfully piloted them to Samuel Cox's house.

Unfortunately, the only way in which Mudd could have disassociated himself from Booth's criminal conspiracy would be by informing the authorities in time to successfully avert the crime. This Mudd could not do. His only chance was the hope that Booth would successfully escape the country, or be killed in the attempt.

Jefferson Davis knew the possible consequences of such a scheme as Booth's. In 1862 when Walker Taylor proposed his plot to Jefferson Davis to capture Lincoln and bring him to Richmond, Davis immediately understood the implications and likely consequences. Lincoln was a courageous man in Davis' own words, and would surely resist capture, making it likely that he might be killed. When one sets out to capture the president of the United States, it is almost certain that someone will die. Mudd's failure to realize this when he willingly embraced Booth's conspiracy to capture showed a serious misjudgment on his part and helped to cast his fate.

What of Lieutenant Lovett's contention that Mudd was evasive in his answers and concealed additional information which he knew was needed? Originally Mudd claimed he did not know Booth, had never met him, and that Booth disguised his appearance by wearing a false beard and hid his face behind a shawl. Mudd further stated that Davy Herold had told him that the two men were headed toward Washington when Booth's horse slipped and fell causing Booth to break his leg. Mudd told Lovett that when the two men left, he directed them to a short cut through the Zekiah Swamp in the direction of Parson Wilmer's (west). This was the opposite direction to the route Booth and Herold actually took. Mudd told Colonel Wells during his interrogation in Bryantown on Friday, April 21, "I have always called myself a Union man." All of the above are at variance with the facts. In each instance, Mudd lied.

That Mudd knew Booth and knew him well is clear from the evidence already discussed. That Booth was disguised so that Mudd did not recognize him is beyond belief. Booth readily identified himself at several stops along his twelve day escape route. He identified himself to Sergeant Cobb at the Navy Yard Bridge. He also identified himself to Samuel Cox, to Thomas A. Jones, Dr. Richard Stuart, and to the three Confederate soldiers that accompanied him across the Rappahannock River on Monday morning, April 24.[12] The only people Booth apparently withheld his identity from were the Garretts when he arrived at their farm on Monday afternoon. If Booth knew Mudd and knew that Mudd knew him, why would Booth seek to disguise himself from the doctor, and more importantly, in seeking medical care, how could he think that he could successfully fool an intelligent clinician like Mudd, who knew him from their three previous meetings?

And lastly, what is Mudd's real connection with St. Mary's Church near Bryantown? Mudd was a member and communicant at St. Peter's Roman Catholic Church a short distance to the east of his farm. He and his wife Sarah were married at St. Peter's and each of his children had been baptized at St. Peter's. St. Peter's is the church of record for Dr. Mudd, and is where he and his family attended services regularly. Yet the two times that Booth visited Dr. Mudd in Charles County, he met him at St. Mary's Church near Bryantown.

Booth's presence at St. Mary's Church in November, and again in December, is testified to by John F. Hardy who places him there on both occasions.[13] St. Mary's was the church of Dr. William Queen, the senior Confederate sympathizer in Charles County, and the man who brought Booth to that church on the two occasions that Dr. Mudd was known to have been there. That Mudd attended St. Mary's Church when Booth was there, furthering his plans, suggests that it was a rendezvous for important members of the Confederate underground. Mudd's presence on the occasion of Booth's two known visits to the church adds further credence to his involvement with Booth, and his plan to capture Lincoln.

When Mudd had successfully cleared his home of Booth and Herold at five o'clock on Saturday evening following his return from Bryantown, he could only hope that they would successfully escape. The best thing that could happen would be for Booth to die before implicating Mudd in his conspiracy. Mudd was caught in a terrible dilemma and all he could do was wait and hope that he would never hear another loud knock on his door in the middle of the night.

WE CANNOT ESCAPE HISTORY.[1]

In a recent biography of Samuel Mudd the author concluded his study with the following observation:

> *This gentle man lived his life well, marred only by some enthusiasms of early adulthood and finally by a sudden unexpected entanglement with an egotistical zealot who had committed a horrendous crime.*[2]

This gentle treatment of Dr. Mudd in which his role in Booth's conspiracy is reduced to an "unexpected entanglement" is consistent with the perception of Mudd for the past one hundred and thirty-plus years. Knowing what the members of the military tribunal knew at the time of the sentencing, life imprisonment for Dr. Mudd was appropriate. Knowing what historians know today, the tribunal would certainly have voted the death sentence for Mudd.[3]

While Mudd's crucial help to Booth did not prevent Booth's ultimate apprehension and death, it did prolong it. More importantly, Mudd's role in the conspiracy to capture not only lent credibility to Booth among key individuals in southern Maryland, but brought two very important members into the plot which eventually involved others. The participation of John Surratt placed a rope around his mother's neck. Even this tragedy has a fine thread which is connected to Mudd.[4]

When all of the evidence is carefully reviewed it is impossible to conclude that this "gentle man's" fate resulted solely from his administration of the Hippocratic oath as his defenders would have us believe. Booth's murder of Lincoln was the crime of the century, and when viewed from the perspective of historical hindsight, it may well have been the crime of the twentieth century as well. Certainly the political events which followed in the wake of Lincoln's death did not bode well for the nation as a whole. It is anyone's guess what course the nation would have followed had Lincoln

The conspirators, from an engraving by A. H. Ritchie in 1865. Conspicuously absent from the ring of conspirators charged by the United States government is the image of Dr. Samuel Alexander Mudd. This omission is found on nearly every composite drawing or photograph illustrating the accused conspirators. While doubts exist among many as to Mary Surratt's guilt, Dr. Mudd has been consistently portrayed as a victim of a hysterical government that rushed to judgment.

survived his theater visit and served out the remaining four years of his presidency.

None of the evidence suggests that Dr. Mudd was knowingly involved in Booth's deliberate act of murder. Mudd probably viewed Lincoln's murder as most intelligent Southerners did, a tragedy for the South. Imagine how Mudd must have felt now that the nation was in the hands of "...cow drivers, pickpockets and gamblers." A people "...so degenerated" that only the "...foreign element" in them allowed them to succeed.

Had the prosecution been aware of Mudd's letter to O. A. Brownson it surely would have used it to discredit him even further, and support the prosecution's contention that Mudd was vehemently anti-Union and sought Lincoln's removal as president. Of course, Mudd's views as expressed in his letter are nothing more than the expressions of a Confederate sympathizer who desired to turn back the clock to the peaceful antebellum days of slavery, but unable to do so because of the policies of Abraham Lincoln.

Mudd was a Southerner who lived by the social and moral standards of the South. He fully supported the Confederate cause, and was surrounded by Confederate sympathizers who actively supported that cause.

As a member of the Confederate mail line which followed one of the routes through southern Maryland (the one ultimately used by Booth in his escape), Mudd came into intimate contact with the key members of the Confederate Signal Service in southern Maryland. These members included Dr. William Queen, John Thompson, Samuel Cox, Thomas Harbin, Thomas Jones and John H. Surratt, Jr.

Perhaps it was only benign circumstances that brought Mudd into contact with Wilkes Booth, but it mattered little what brought the two together initially. The acquaintance, once made, was enough to eventually lead to Mudd's undoing. Mudd and Booth were believers in a cause that demanded the removal of Lincoln—one way or another.

That John Wilkes Booth was introduced to Dr. Mudd at St. Mary's Church in November by Dr. William Queen's son-in-law, John Thompson, was not the result of good manners following church services. Booth's visit later in December to the Mudd house, and his overnight stay were crucial to Booth's ultimate plans. The question is, why did Dr. Queen pass Booth along to Dr. Mudd of all people in southern Maryland? The answer must lie in Mudd's role, and his reliability as a key contact in Queen's eyes.

Mudd's subsequent role in arranging a meeting in which he introduced Booth to Thomas Harbin and still later, when he introduced John Surratt to Booth, played a crucial part in Booth's scheme to capture—then murder—President Lincoln. Mudd may well have been reluctant, even adamant, about involving himself with a man like Booth in his dangerous scheme to capture the president. But involve himself he did and while his involvement may be viewed as trivial by some, it proved crucial to Booth.

Mudd knew that it was John Wilkes Booth who came to his door on that fateful Saturday morning of April 15, 1865, and when confronted with the shocking news in Bryantown on Saturday afternoon that Lincoln had been killed by Booth at Ford's Theatre, he was caught in a terrible trap. Once aware of the situation, he did the only thing he could do to save his own neck. He returned home and told Booth to leave, and to avoid Federal troops by skirting around Bryantown. Having sent Booth off with a fore-warning, Mudd could only wait and hope for the best. In his own mind he knew he would never have involved himself in Booth's murder scheme. To the very end Mudd maintained his innocence, claiming to be a victim of a hysterical and vengeful government. While the government may have been hysterical and vengeful, it is hard to picture Mudd as a victim.

Since Dr. Mudd's death in 1883, a rising force has made its way into the cultural history of the country in an effort to reverse the role attributed to Mudd in the assassination of Abraham Lincoln. The first major effort of any wide standing was the biography of Samuel Mudd written by his youngest child, Nettie Mudd Monroe.[5]   Only five years old at the time of her father's death, Nettie gleaned much of her information from her mother who lived until 1911. Nettie published her book in 1906 when she was twenty-eight years old and her mother was seventy-one. At the time of its publication the book was well received, but had limited distribution. Today, the original edition is found mostly in private libraries as a scarce collectible.

In 1936, a movie was made about Dr. Mudd by Twentieth Century Fox studio under the direction of John Ford entitled *The Prisoner of Shark Island*. The film, starring the talented Warner Baxter, was well received, and al-most overnight Samuel Mudd became a folk hero. The film was classic Hollywood, and stressed the theme of a mild-mannered country doctor who sought only to extend his healing powers to a sick and injured stranger. As a result of his good Samaritan efforts, Dr. Mudd was swept up in the military's dragnet and ruthlessly rushed to judgment by a vengeful and retribution-seeking government.

Pronounced guilty by a kangaroo court, Dr. Mudd was clandestinely shipped to Fort Jefferson on the Dry Tortugas, called Shark Island in the movie. Here Mudd spent the next three and a half years alternating be-tween physical abuse and mental torture. Not the least of Mudd's troubles, according to the Hollywood version, were large man-eating sharks that constantly circled within the prison moat ensuring a horrible death to all those who tried to escape.

While *The Prisoner of Shark Island* was more Hollywood fiction than fact, it was a well-made movie drama that focused people's attention on the Lincoln assassination and the Mudd story.

In 1995, Light Vision Films produced a documentary video tape en-titled, *Rewriting History: The Case of Dr. Samuel A. Mudd*. This eighty-minute documentary claims to examine, "...the hysteria and shock of 1865," and asks, "Was Dr. Mudd wrongfully tried and imprisoned?" In support of the video's thesis, several notables render their opinions on the innocence of Dr. Mudd, and the illegal jurisdiction of the military commission that tried him. Unfortunately, the documentary does not discuss the great body of evidence against Dr. Mudd nor does it offer any explanation of most of the events and statements raised in the current work and well-known to several of the experts who provided commentary in the video. Like *The Prisoner of Shark Island*, the documentary is a successful presentation of the views expressed by members of the Mudd family and other defenders of Dr. Mudd.[6]

One of the more egregious falsehoods that continues to permeate the accounts of Mudd's treatment by the government is that Mudd, along with the other male conspirators, was forced to wear a canvas hood by order of Secretary of War Edwin M. Stanton. Mudd was said to have endured this "...especially vicious torture" while in his prison cell.[7] His eyes and ears were covered with cotton, and the hood, which extended to mid-waist, was tied tightly about his neck and waist. He could not see or hear. He was held completely incommunicado as a result of this diabolical treatment.

According to one author, "...No explanation was given for this treatment...."[8] Perhaps no explanation was given because Mudd was never treated in such a manner. It is one more distortion in the story of Mudd.

The prisoners, including Dr. Mudd, were held at the Washington Penitentiary on the arsenal grounds in the District of Columbia in specially prepared cells under the command of Major General John F. Hartranft. Hartranft reported directly to his commanding officer, Major General Winfield Scott Hancock. Hancock had heard that Hartranft was granting Mudd special privileges as a result of Mudd being seated in the courtroom separately from the other prisoners who were confined in an area behind a low railing. In response to Hancock's request for an explanation of Mudd's seating arrangement, Hartranft wrote the following communiqué to Hancock:

> Hd. Qrs. Mil. Prison
> Wash. Arsenal. May 10th 1865
> 9:40 P.M.

> Major Genl. Hancock
> Comdg. Mid. Mil. Div.
> General,
>
> In reply to your communication relative to my giving especial privileges to Dr. Mudd, I respectfully state that the separation of Dr. Mudd from the rest of the prisoners was accidental and occurred as follows:
>
> On Tuesday, when the prisoners were taken into Court, Dr. Mudd and Mrs. Surratt happened to be the last of the prisoners brought in; the

other six were taken into the prisoners' dock and by seating the person in charge of each prisoner by his side, the room was all taken up. When the Dr. was brought in, he was placed on a chair, just in front of the other prisoners and outside of the railing. Mrs. Surratt was also seated near him.

To day the prisoners were brought in and seated in the same manner, I thinking that it would be more convenient for the Court to have them seated the same each day.

*Dr. Mudd has been treated since he has been in this prison, precisely the same as each of the other male prisoners, except that **he has not been hooded, which was in accordance with your instructions**.*

I disclaim all intention of granting Dr. Mudd any privileges.

I have the honor to be

> *Very Respectfully*
> *Your Obt. Scrvt.*
> *Bvt. Maj. Genl.*
> *Gov. and Comdr. Mil. Prison.[9]*

Hartranft's statement belies the persistent claim in numerous works that Dr. Mudd was hooded. The claim that Mudd was hooded, however, casts further suspicion on the behavior of the military tribunal.

Over the next several decades following *Shark Island*, historical writings picked up the theme of Mudd's innocence and brutal handling by the government with a seeming ignorance of much of the evidence surrounding

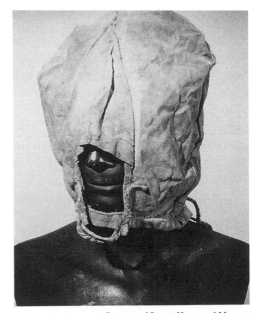

One of the hoods worn by the accused during their initial incarceration.

Courtesy of Surratt House and Museum

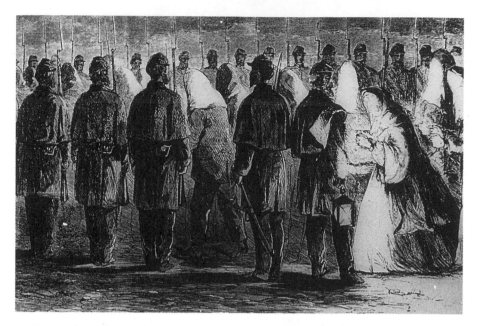

Engraving of prisoners being led from their cells showing use of hoods. Engraving from **Frank Leslie's Magazine, 1865.** *While many have written that Mudd was hooded during his early confinement, Major General John F. Hartranft, in charge of the prison and prisoners, wrote to his commanding officer, Major General Winfield Scott Hancock that Mudd, "...has not been hooded, which was in accordance with your instructions."*

Mudd's role in Booth's original conspiracy and subsequent escape. Despite the sympathetic treatment which Mudd generally received in historical treatises of the period, no serious effort existed to reverse the judgment of the court. This came later as a result of Mudd's grandson, Dr. Richard Dyer Mudd,[10] who mounted a campaign to "free" his grandfather as early as the administration of Franklin D. Roosevelt. Richard Mudd's attempts to seek presidential intervention on his grandfather's behalf met with repeated frustration. A measure of success did not come until the administration of Jimmy Carter.[11]

On July 24, 1979, President Jimmy Carter wrote a letter to Dr. Richard Mudd in support of his efforts on behalf of his grandfather, and of Carter's belief that his grandfather was innocent. Carter wrote that while he, as president, was unable to set aside Dr. Samuel Mudd's conviction, he agreed fully with President Andrew Johnson's statements in his pardon of Mudd. In particular, Carter quoted the following from Johnson's pardon:

...it is represented to me by intelligent and respectable members of the medical profession that the circumstances of the surgical aid to the escaping of the assassin and the imputed concealment of his flight are deserving of a lenient construction, as within the obligations of professional duty and, thus, inadequate evidence of a guilty sympathy with the crime or the criminal;

And ...in other respects the evidence, imputing such guilty sympathy or purpose of aid in defeat of justice, leaves room for uncertainty as to the true measure and nature of the complicity of the said Samuel A. Mudd in the attempted escape of said assassins ...

Carter concluded his letter with the following statement:

A careful reading of the information provided to me about this case led to my personal agreement with the findings of President Johnson. I am hopeful that these conclusions will be given widespread circulation which will restore dignity to your grandfather's name and clear the Mudd family name of any negative connotation or implied lack of honor.

When Dr. Mudd was offered and accepted a full and unconditional pardon on February 8, 1869, by President Johnson, the case of presidential exoneration or reversal of guilt was closed. As President Carter states, perhaps for the first time in the long history of efforts to exonerate Samuel Mudd,

All legal authority vested in the President to act in this case was exercised when President Andrew Johnson granted Dr. Mudd a full and unconditional pardon on February 8, 1869.

After nearly seventy years of continuous effort to "free" his grandfather, Richard Mudd was greatly heartened and pleased with President Carter's gracious letter.[12] The news media quickly followed up on the release of the letter, and declared that Dr. Samuel Mudd had finally been exonerated and declared innocent of any wrong doing by the president of the United States. Of course, Carter did no such thing. As he clearly states in his letter, all presidential authority was exercised by Andrew Johnson in 1869. President Carter merely added the considerable weight of his position at the time to express his personal opinion that,

...a careful reading of the information provided to me about this case led to my personal agreement with the findings of President Johnson.

Clearly Presidents Andrew Johnson and Jimmy Carter did not have all of the information provided to them when they concluded that,

...Dr. Mudd's guilt was limited to aiding the escape of President Lincoln's assassins and did not involve any other participation or complicity in the assassination plot itself....[13]

Not to be outdone by President Carter, President Ronald Reagan, on December 8, 1987, wrote to Dr. Richard Mudd extending his support on behalf of Dr. Mudd's grandfather.[14]   Like Carter before him, Reagan lamented his inability to do anything further on behalf of Samuel Mudd and concluded his letter by stating the obvious:

> But we'll have to accept that 'full unconditional pardon' is what we must settle for.

While Dr. Richard Mudd's initial reaction to President Carter's letter (and President Reagan's eight years later) was that the curtain was finally closing on his years of struggle to gain a presidential reversal of the military tribunal's action, the curtain was suddenly raised yet one more time.

On January 22, 1992, a hearing was obtained before the Army Board for the Correction of Military Records (ABCMR). This board consists of civilian members that hear claims concerning military records that are believed to be in error, and makes recommendations to the secretary of the army based on its findings. The board lacks any authority to change any record, but acting on evidence presented and reviewed, comes to its recommendations which it submits to the secretary of the army.[15]

Because of its nature, the board hears evidence only from the aggrieved parties as to the claim of error in the record. Lawyers representing the Mudd family together with family members were allowed to appear before the board and present their evidence. Opponents to the petition to correct or expunge the record were not allowed to appear before the board and present counter evidence. An examiner acting for the board presents the facts and relevant law in question to the board. The board may, and frequently does, put questions to the examiner as to the relevant law in the case.

The arguments presented to the board by the proponents stated that no basis existed in 1865 for the military jurisdiction over the accused Dr. Samuel A. Mudd.[16] On questioning, the examiner recommended that Samuel Mudd (and his family) be granted relief. It is important to note that the board did not consider the question of Dr. Mudd's innocence or guilt—only whether he was lawfully tried by a military commission.

The board heard the arguments and agreed with the court appointed examiner that relief be granted to the Mudd family in the case of Dr. Samuel A. Mudd. In its conclusion the board stated:

> ...the board finds no good reason why Dr. Mudd should not have been tried by a civilian court. It, therefore, unanimously concludes that the military commission did not have jurisdiction to try him, and that in so doing denied him his due process rights, particularly his right to trial by a jury of his peers. This denial constituted such a gross infringement of his Constitutionally protected rights, that his conviction should be set aside.[17]

When the board found "...no good reason why Dr. Mudd should not have been tried by a civilian court" it ignored the rulings by the Attorney General of the United States, James Speed, in 1865, and Federal District Court Judge Thomas Jefferson Boynton who presided over the District Court for the United States of the Southern District of Florida in 1867. Both Speed and Boynton ruled that the military commission had legal jurisdiction to try the accused conspirators. (These rulings are covered in detail in Chapter 10.)

The board's recommendation was forwarded to the secretary of the army's designee, William D. Clark, acting Assistant Secretary of the Army. Secretary Clark, in reviewing the record, denied the recommendation of the board. In his ruling, Clark wrote:

> *The ABCMR concluded that the military commission which tried Dr. Mudd did not have jurisdiction over civilians and recommended that Dr. Mudd's conviction be set aside on that basis.*
>
> *Accordingly, my denial of that recommendation **should not be taken as a determination of either the guilt or the innocence of Dr. Mudd.** It is not the role of the ABCMR to attempt to settle historical disputes. Neither is the ABCMR an appellate court. The precise issue which the ABCMR proposes to decide, **the jurisdiction of the military commission over Dr. Mudd, was specifically addressed at the time in two separate habeas corpus proceedings, one before the Chief Justice of the Supreme Court, the other before a U.S. District Court. There also was an opinion by the Attorney General of the United States.***
>
> *The effect of the action recommended by the ABCMR would be to overrule all those determinations. Even if the issue might be decided differently today, it is inappropriate for a non-judicial body, such as the ABCMR, to declare that the law 127 years ago was contrary to what was determined contemporarily by prominent legal authorities.*
>
> *Accordingly, I have rejected the ABCMR's recommendations and have denied the application for relief.*[18]

It is a wonder how the Army Board for Correction of Military Records was ever allowed to hear the petition in the first place based upon Clark's ruling. To plead the lack of legal jurisdiction of the military commission whereby the ruling declares that the ABCMR has no authority as a board to overrule judicial rulings seems to preclude its authority from the very beginning.

Nonetheless, this hearing is instructive to students of the conspiracy trial. It brings legally trained experts into the arena previously held almost exclusively by non-legally trained historians.

While Assistant Secretary of the Army Clark was still deliberating over the board's assessment of the hearing, and before his ruling, the University of Richmond School of Law, with the approval of Dr. Richard Mudd, staged a moot court in which a full adversarial hearing was held on the question of Mudd's trial. The school proposed an appellate hearing with experienced jurists trained in the law. This moot court brought the question of Mudd's trial even closer to professional legal scholarship.

Representing the defendant, Dr. Mudd, was the great-great-granddaughter of Brigadier General Thomas Ewing, Jr., who originally defended Dr. Mudd in 1865.[19]

The panel of judges listened to and asked numerous questions of the advocates for each side after which they deliberated and rendered a unanimous opinion. The three judges agreed in their verdict that the military commission lacked legal jurisdiction to try and convict Dr. Mudd. Interestingly, while the panel sat in judgment deliberating only on the question of the legal jurisdiction of the military commission, all three judges could not resist discussing the innocence of the defendant in their findings, leading us to believe that the historical intrigue surrounding Mudd is impossible to ignore even among leading jurists.

Unfortunately, it would seem that once again, the question of whether the military tribunal that tried Dr. Mudd had legal jurisdiction cannot be separated from the question of his guilt or innocence. Would the panel of judges have ruled otherwise if they were firmly convinced of Mudd's guilt? Presumably, they would still have ruled against the jurisdiction of the military commission, but one wonders.

These two quasi-legal events are carefully presented in a recent publication together with five commentaries by eminent scholars in support of one position or the other.[20] The student of the legal aspects of the Lincoln assassination and the military tribunal that followed it will find substantial grist from among these excellent writings.[21]

As the curtain was finally descending following these latest efforts to "free Dr. Mudd," it suddenly was raised one more time. On June 12, 1997, Congressman Steny Hoyer (D., Maryland 5th) with co-sponsor Thomas Ewing (R., Illinois 15th) introduced a bill into the House of Representatives seeking relief for Dr. Mudd.[22] The bill directs "...the Secretary of the Army to set aside the conviction of Dr. Samuel A. Mudd by a military commission in 1865 for aiding, abetting, and assisting the conspirators who assassinated President Abraham Lincoln."[23] The bill's findings state that:

> The conviction of Dr. Mudd was based on evidence of guilt that fell so far short of meeting the prosecution's burden of proof that such conviction amounted to a denial of due process of law which was so extreme as to constitute fundamental unfairness.
>
> Because the conviction of Dr. Mudd was not based on sufficient evidence and resulted in a denial of due process of law, the Secretary of the Army should set aside the conviction.[24]

In his remarks from the floor of the House, Mr. Hoyer stated:

> *Mr. Speaker, while it is clear that Dr. Mudd did set John Wilkes Booth's broken leg, there is absolutely no evidence to suggest that he was either a co-conspirator in the assassination of President Lincoln or even aware of the events which had occurred earlier that evening on Friday, April 14, 1865.*
>
> *I urge my colleagues to join me in ensuring that history is recorded accurately and that our Nation's most basic individual rights, embodied in the Constitution, are not violated at any time. Dr. Samuel Mudd's name and honor and that of his family, many of whom live in my district, hang in the balance. We ought to allow the findings and decision of the Army Board for Correction of Military Records, the most reputable and qualified entity to date which has reviewed this case, to stand, thus ending the 132-year-long disservice accorded to Dr. Samuel Mudd.*

Congressman Hoyer's remarks reflect the ongoing effort to revise the history of this sad epoch in our nation's past. Clearly Mr. Hoyer and the Army Board for Correction of Military Records (ABCMR) have not availed themselves of the primary source documents, including the statements of Dr. Samuel A. Mudd himself, which are readily available in this case. The failure of these two important entities to carefully review the entire judicial record before attempting to revise history is indefensible. The effort by the Legislative Branch to overturn the rulings of the Judicial Branch is without precedent, and amounts to an attempt to alter legal history by non-judicial means.

The best argument against such legislative tampering can be found in a letter by assassination historian James O. Hall to the editor of the *Maryland Independent*:

> *Perhaps it would be best for Congressman Hoyer to withdraw H. R. 1885 and leave the matter of Dr. Mudd's guilt or innocence to competent researchers and historians. They will have the last word anyway.*[25]

As the debate over the lawful jurisdiction of the military tribunal and the guilt or innocence of Dr. Mudd thickens, a clearer, more objective understanding of those momentous events surrounding the terrible death of Abraham Lincoln should eventually emerge.

The tendency of many writers and politicians to gloss over the role of Dr. Mudd[26] is no longer acceptable to students of the assassination. A more demanding review of the participants and events of that time is now being made. To accept Samuel Mudd as simply the good doctor who was victimized by an insane zealot is too simplistic and historically remiss. At some point, when all of the emotion is past, the whole truth will finally emerge. As Abraham Lincoln so astutely observed in the fall of 1862, *We cannot escape history.*

9

THE GOOD DOCTOR

Samuel Alexander Mudd (1833-1883) was born on December 20, 1833 at Oak Hill, the farm of his father, Henry Lowe Mudd, Sr. The senior Mudd's farm was located a short distance from the site of what would become Mudd's own farm in 1859.[1] Henry Mudd was a farmer of substantial means in Charles County, Maryland, where he owned several hundred acres of farm land along with several slaves needed to provide the considerable labor required for culturing tobacco. By the outbreak of the Civil War, tobacco was second only to cotton among the South's most profitable agricultural crops.

Henry Mudd was a strong advocate of education, and through a combination of public, private and home schooling, provided substantially for young Sam Mudd's schooling. At the age of seven, Sam attended public school for two years after which his father hired a tutor to teach his children at home. At fourteen years of age Sam attended the St. John's College in Frederick, Maryland where he received his first formal classical education. It was while at St. John's that young Sam met his future wife, Sarah Frances Dyer (1835-1911), who became known as "Frank" to Sam and his family.[2]

Sarah Dyer was attending a girl's academy in Frederick at the same time Sam was attending St. John's College. Following his course of instruction at St. John's, Sam returned home to Charles County only to leave shortly afterwards, and enroll in Georgetown College in the District of Columbia. Sam studied at Georgetown for three years, from 1850 to 1853. Shortly after returning home, Sam decided that his real interest lay more in medicine than farming. Under the able mentoring of his second cousin, Dr. George Mudd, he entered the Baltimore Medical College (later to become the University of Maryland Medical School) where he completed two years of medical training and received his certification to practice medicine as an M.D. in 1856.

Mudd's acquaintance with Sarah Dyer during the period they both attended school in Frederick blossomed into a courtship, which led to Mudd asking Sarah to marry him. Both Sam and Sarah were still in their teens when Sam proposed marriage, and Sarah told Sam that she would marry him, but not before he finished his education, and earned his medical degree. Sam agreed.

Having successfully graduated from Baltimore Medical College in 1856, Sam and Sarah were married on November 26, 1857 and set up housekeeping in the home of Sarah's brother, Jeremiah Dyer, who was a bachelor at the time.[3] Within the year, Sam and Frank purchased 218 acres from the original patent granted to Thomas Mudd, the progenitor of the Maryland Mudds. Sam then set about to have their own house built on the newly acquired tract, known as St. Catharine's. St. Catharine's traced its lineage back to Thomas Mudd in the year 1696, and at the time Sam acquired St. Catharine's, it had descended through the Mudd family for nearly one hundred and sixty-two years.[4]

While Sam and Frank waited for their new house to be built, their first child, Andrew Jerome, was born in November 1858. In 1859, the three Mudds moved into their newly-constructed home and Sam took up the dual role of farmer-doctor. Over the next six years, three more children were born to the couple: Lillian Augusta (June 2, 1860), Thomas Dyer (June 6, 1861),[5] and Samuel Alexander II (January 30, 1864). For the next thirteen and a half months, Sam and Frank and their four children would lead happy normal lives in the midst of family and friends in the rural southern community of Charles County, Maryland.

A Southerner by heritage and tradition, Samuel Mudd continued the life of a Southern planter and part-time physician that was a natural way of life among his peers. At one point, Mudd owned as many as eleven slaves who provided the labor for his tobacco farm, not always under happy circumstances.

During the trial of Dr. Mudd, the prosecution introduced six of his former slaves as witnesses against him.[6] The prosecution introduced these witnesses in an effort to show the court that Mudd had frequently harbored and cared for Confederate soldiers at his home, and secreted soldiers at various times in the woods near his house, supplying them with blankets and food.[7] The conclusion which the prosecution attempted to make to the court was that Mudd was more than a Confederate sympathizer; he was an active player in the rebellion.

During the testimony of Elzee Eglen, one of Mudd's former slaves, Eglen told of being shot by Mudd because he had not responded quickly enough to Mudd's orders.[8] Eglen was described during the trial as being "obstreperous." Clearly Mudd did not want to kill Eglen, but only wound him as a lesson for Eglen's tardiness in responding to his instructions. Other slaves testified to being whipped by him.[9] These incidents, along with the vituperations in his letter to Orestes Brownson and Mudd's derogatory references to blacks in his letters home while imprisoned, seldom appear in the numerous treatises about the doctor. By any standard, owning slaves and whipping and shooting them seems at variance with the ideals of the Hippocratic oath.

That Mudd was an educated man, a pious man and a respected care-giver among the citizens of Charles County is certain. But Mudd was also a man whose principles fully encompassed the Southern ideal that states' rights included the right of select individuals to declare certain other people as non-citizens whose status was only as property. Mudd strongly de-fended that principle and, like most of his neighbors with the exception of his mentor Dr. George Mudd, he supported the use of arms against his countrymen to preserve that principle.

Mudd's principles as a physician and a practitioner of the Hippocratic oath were at variance with his actions in support of the Southern cause. If he objected to anything involving the plot to capture Lincoln and change the course of the war, it was not the plot itself so much as the plotters. Booth and his band of cohorts were not of Mudd's ilk. But John Wilkes Booth had apparently used the right names in drawing Mudd into his scheme.

The government sentence of life imprisonment was a devastating blow to Mudd. His only hope of keeping his sanity in light of such a sentence lay in his belief that friends and family would be able to reverse the tribunal's ruling or at least gain a presidential pardon.

The military tribunal sentenced four of the accused conspirators to death by hanging: Mary Surratt, Lewis Powell, Davy Herold and George Atzerodt. Three were sentenced to life imprisonment: Samuel Mudd, Samuel Arnold and Michael O' Laughlen. Edman Spangler received a six-year sentence.[10] The death sentences were carried out on the arsenal grounds next to the very building where the prisoners had been incarcerated and tried. The remaining four were originally scheduled for imprisonment at the federal penitentiary at Albany, New York, but this was quickly changed to Fort Jefferson in the Dry Tortugas.

Fort Jefferson was the most remote of all federal forts within the juris-diction of the United States, located approximately seventy miles off of Key West, Florida in the Gulf of Mexico. Some have speculated that the change was made by Stanton to keep the convicted men under military control and as remote from family and friends as possible. This speculation is consis-tent with Stanton's behavior and his authority at the time. If Stanton had wanted to isolate the prisoners within the military system, no better place existed than Fort Jefferson.

Mudd arrived at the fort near the end of July 1865, after a two week journey aboard a federal steamship. Life for Dr. Mudd at Dry Tortugas was varied over the next three and a half years of his imprisonment. Initially, Mudd was treated without deference to his professional position and training and served as a prison laborer.

Two months after he began serving his sentence, Mudd attempted to escape the island fortress by stowing away in the hold of one of the supply ships that infrequently stopped at the fort. Discovered, Mudd was treated harshly at first, confined in chains, and kept in a communal cell with several other prisoners—treatment not unusual for an attempted escapee.[11] The harsh treatment was short-lived, however, as Mudd himself described in one of his many letters home. In a letter dated October 5, 1865, ten days after his abortive escape attempt, Mudd wrote to his brother-in-law, Jeremiah Dyer:

> I am taking my present hardship as a joke. I am not put back in the least. I will soon assume my former position, or one equally respectable. The only thing connected with my present attitude is the name, and not the reality. I have no labor to perform, yet I am compelled to answer roll-call, and to sleep in the guard house at night. This will not last longer than this week.[12]

Meanwhile, life back on the farm was increasingly difficult for Mrs. Mudd and her four children. Much is made of Frank's plight who, left husbandless with her four children, was faced with the task of maintaining the farm in Sam's absence. She did have help, however. Jere Dyer, Frank's brother, assumed responsibility for overseeing the farm operation and Sarah certainly had Sam's father and his labor force to help make sure the farm continued to function and that Frank and her children were provided for.[13]

As time distanced the failed escape attempt, Mudd was assigned to the carpenter's shop at the prison. While it is not clear precisely what his official duties were within the prison shop, it is clear that Mudd had time to practice the art of cabinetry. Among the items which the family descendants proudly cite in their inventory of Mudd prison artifacts are a "ladies work box," an "inlaid center table," a presentation "cane," "wreaths and flowers made of collected shells," and several "cribbage boards."[14] At least Mudd's incarceration offered some intellectual stimulation and was not so harsh as to leave him debilitated and unable to fashion cabinetry.[15]

Dr. Mudd's first major break came in June 1867 with the outbreak of yellow fever at the fort. Although a life-threatening scourge, the fever proved a life saver to Mudd. A parasitic disease carried by the mosquito, yellow fever can often prove fatal. Within weeks scores of inhabitants at the fort came down with the disease. The only physician at the fort was Dr. Joseph Sim Smith, a Union surgeon who had been a classmate of Mudd's at Georgetown College.

Military tribunal and government prosecutors.

The last vestige of the old Washington Arsenal where the accused were tried. The trial was held on the third floor of the present building which has survived as an apartment building for officers at Fort Lesley McNair.

The final judgment. Of the ten individuals found guilty by the government, four were sentenced to hang: Mary Surratt, Powell, Herold and Atzerodt.

Fort Jefferson. Of the remaining six conspirators, four were sentenced to prison in Fort Jefferson: Mudd, O'Laughlen, Arnold and Spangler; Booth being dead and John Surratt still at large.

Smith arrived at the island shortly after the outbreak and was soon overwhelmed by the spread of the disease. He wisely enlisted the aid of his old school mate, Dr. Mudd. Within six weeks Dr. Smith and his young son were dead, leaving a widow and young daughter stranded on the island and surrounded by the yellow death.[16]

On Smith's death, Dr. Mudd assumed medical responsibility for the remaining inhabitants at the fort until aid came in the person of Dr. D. W. Whitehurst, a Key West surgeon. The two physicians labored day and night to care for the victims of the disease, but there was little that medicine could do other than attempt to relieve some of the symptoms. Medical science had not yet learned that the disease was transmitted by the mosquito and even if the islanders had known that fact there is little they could have done to eradicate the infestation that swept over the island.

Among those who fell victim to the fever were Sam Arnold and Michael O'Laughlen, Mudd's fellow conspirators. Arnold eventually recovered, but O'Laughlen died. Mudd himself eventually contracted the fever, but with care recovered in time to see the last of the epidemic blow out to sea.

As a result of Mudd's humanitarian efforts, he was given free run of the fort. A petition was signed by all of the inhabitants of the fort in support of Mudd for his heroic efforts, but the petition failed to reach the president. A new commandant arrived who returned the fort to its previous conditions, leaving Mudd in deep despair to ponder his ultimate fate.

Then, in February 1869, President Andrew Johnson issued a presidential pardon freeing Mudd "unconditionally."[17] Within two weeks, both Arnold and Spangler received similar pardons.[18]

Mudd returned home to his wife and four children and began to pick up the pieces. Over the next several years Sarah and Sam had five more children;[19] Sam resumed his farming and medical practice; and eventually he ran for the state legislature. In 1877, Mudd ran as a delegate for the state legislature along with his neighbor, Samuel Cox, Jr. The good people of Charles County saw fit to elect Cox, Jr. as their delegate while sending Dr. Mudd back home.

During the fourteen years following his release from imprisonment Mudd maintained a low profile, save for his one attempt at elective office. He maintained his innocence whenever pressed to comment on the momentous events surrounding Lincoln's death. In the end, his devotion to his medical practice is said to have resulted in his death. While administering to his patients in January 1883, Dr. Mudd contracted pneumonia and on January 10, 1883, at the age of 49, died. He was laid to rest in the church cemetery next to the building where he first met with John Wilkes Booth on that fateful Sunday in November 1864—St. Mary's Catholic Church.

10

INTER ARMA SILENT LEGES[1]

According to Colonel Wells' testimony, Mudd had undergone several interviews beginning on Tuesday, April 18 and ending on Sunday, April 23. After interviewing Mudd on Friday, April 21, Wells, now convinced of Mudd's duplicity, had his house staked out by troopers. On Sunday morning, Wells personally visited the Mudd farm and had Mudd show him the route the two fugitives took when they left on Saturday evening. Mudd pointed out tracks leading away from the rear of his house in the direction of the Zekiah Swamp.

Wells was satisfied that Mudd was lying about his relationship with Booth and his own role in Lincoln's murder. He was convinced that Mudd not only knew where Booth and Herold were hiding out, but that Mudd was rendering Booth medical assistance. On Monday morning, April 24, Wells sent a troop of cavalry to Mudd's house to arrest him and take him to Washington for further questioning. By now, the authorities had seven of the ten alleged conspirators in custody. Only Booth, Herold and John Surratt were still at large. Within forty eight hours Booth and Herold would be in custody leaving only John Surratt still free.[2]

Satisfied of Mudd's complicity in Booth's plot, the government charged Mudd as a conspirator in the murder of Abraham Lincoln. Also charged were seven other individuals (Booth being dead and Surratt still at large).

On May 1, 1865, President Andrew Johnson issued an Executive Order[3] directing that those accused in the former president's murder stand trial before a military commission composed of nine Union officers.[4] After seven weeks of hearings the commission handed down its rulings finding all eight individuals guilty. Four were sentenced to death by hanging (Mary Surratt, Lewis Powell, David Herold and George Atzerodt), three were sentenced to life imprisonment (Samuel Mudd, Samuel Arnold and Michael O'Laughlen), and one was sentenced to six years' imprisonment (Edman Spangler).

On July 7, 1865, the four conspirators sentenced to death were hanged on a special gallows constructed within the walls of the arsenal in the District of Columbia. Mudd, along with Arnold, O'Laughlen and Spangler were ordered transferred to the military prison at Fort Jefferson. With the conclusion of that final act, the punishments meted out by the military commission which had been charged with "removing the stain of innocent blood from the land"[5] became a matter of controversy that still swirls about the heads of historians and students alike.

Defenders of Mudd, as well as most writers on the subject, maintain that the military tribunal of 1865 was illegal and that Mudd was improperly tried and convicted. Unfortunately, the controversy surrounding the legality of the trial is often confused with the question of Mudd's guilt or innocence. The principal question arising from this unique episode is whether the military commission was a properly constituted body which had legal authority to try, convict and sentence the accused conspirators in the murder of Abraham Lincoln. Those who answer against the commission's authority cite as their principal justification for claiming its illegal basis the Supreme Court decision of 1866 known as *ex parte Milligan*.[6]

The serious student of the Lincoln assassination can readily cite this landmark decision in which the Supreme Court ruled that the military commission was without jurisdiction in those districts removed from military zones in which the civil courts were open and functioning and where no threat of military action existed. This ruling has been used by scholars and students alike as a blanket condemnation of the military commission that tried the Lincoln conspirators, and thus brand the commission that tried them as illegal. But is it so?

While the Supreme Court never issued a decision on the tribunal's jurisdiction in the cases of Mudd and his co-defendants, it did hear a petition on their behalf. In February 1869, the Supreme Court agreed to listen to arguments on behalf of Arnold and Spangler (Mudd had been pardoned only days before). The court heard oral arguments but issued no decision since Johnson preempted the court by pardoning both petitioners before the court could rule, leaving the question moot.[7]

Since that time, however, a series of rulings have been issued which bear on this question and warrant our review. In attempting to arrive at a conclusion concerning the status of the commission, however, we need to reach back to those opening days of the rebellion. This was a time when constitutional questions and civil liberties were being subjected to a series of executive actions which ultimately led to the commission's existence and sanction.

If the days between Lincoln's election and his inauguration were full of strife and discord, the ones immediately following were even more so. Lincoln's dilemma was to do everything within his power to avoid war without ensuring the permanency of secession. It was a precarious balancing act which was predestined to failure.

Acts of open hostility against the federal government increased with alarming frequency until open warfare finally erupted with the Confederate bombardment of Fort Sumter. Ten days later, Federal troops were involved in open rioting on the streets of Baltimore within forty miles of the national capital.

Experiencing increasing difficulty and frustration in dealing with individuals and groups opposed to the government's efforts to suppress the rebellion, Lincoln decided to move quickly to render harmless those people whom he deemed detrimental to the Union cause. On April 25, 1861, he issued an order to the commanding general of the army, Winfield Scott, authorizing Scott to suspend the privilege of the writ of habeas corpus along certain military lines, but only under the "extremist necessity."[8] Within two days, on April 27, Lincoln issued a second, similar order to Scott authorizing him to suspend the writ, "if necessary" along the military line from Philadelphia to Washington.[9]

Lincoln desperately needed troops and, having the experience of Baltimore on April 19 fresh in his mind, he meant to obtain them as quickly as possible without further hindrance. He had seized upon the opportunity of suspending the writ of habeas corpus as a military necessity. In the eyes of Lincoln and many of his supporters, civil processes were becoming increasingly ineffective. The increasing number of arrests for treason and the growing failures to stem the tide of opposition caused federal authorities to lose confidence in the courts, and to turn to the military, especially in areas where Southern sympathies ran high.

In suspending the writ of habeas corpus, Lincoln contended that he was authorized by the constitutional provision which states in part, "The privilege of the Writ of Habeas Corpus shall not be suspended unless when in Cases of Rebellion or Invasion the Public Safety may require it."[10] Lincoln interpreted this to mean that the president was empowered to suspend the writ if and when he deemed the safety to be in jeopardy.

Censure of Lincoln's action was immediate. Controversy swirled about the embattled president and his orders limiting civil liberties. His first hard test arose in a confrontation with the venerable eighty-four year old Supreme Court Chief Justice, Roger Brooke Taney.

On May 25, 1861, a troop of Pennsylvania militia had arrested a prominent Marylander named John B. Merryman in the early morning hours at his Cockeysville home. Merryman, whose sympathies and militant actions were clearly against the national government, was taken to Baltimore where he was confined in the military prison at Fort McHenry.

Merryman, an astute lawyer, immediately petitioned for his release on a writ of habeas corpus before Judge Taney who was then sitting as a circuit court judge for the District of Baltimore.[11] Taney promptly issued the writ ordering the military commander of the district, Major General George B. Cadwallader, to deliver Merryman to the court immediately. General Cadwallader asked Taney for more time so that he might consult with his commander-in-chief as to whether he should comply with the judge's order. Taney answered by sending the marshal for the District of Baltimore to Fort McHenry with orders to arrest Cadwallader on contempt charges. The marshal was met at the gates of the fort by an armed guard which refused his admittance, forcing him to return to Taney empty-handed. The military had stood down the prestigious chief justice, and old Taney knew exactly where to level his wrath.

On the 28th of May the aging Taney strode into an overflowing courtroom to tumultuous cheers and delivered a stinging oration. In his castigation of the newly elected president, Taney traced the history of the writ down through English common law to the U.S. Constitution, sharply pointing out that the president of the United States had no authority whatsoever to suspend this sacred and valuable right. He further admonished Lincoln by reminding him of his oath to uphold the Constitution and the law of the land, and directed him to start doing so now.

But outwitting Lincoln, as Taney and the rest of the country would soon learn, was no easy task. Sensing the difficulty of his position and realizing that he could gain little and lose much in a jousting match with the wily chief justice, Lincoln pocketed the judge's ruling and held his silence. Taney had had his day in court but lost to Lincoln and the weight of arms.

During the next year and a half Lincoln suspended the writ on five separate occasions, each time specifying special and narrow circumstances.[12] Then on September 24, 1862, he issued a sweeping order in which, "...all Rebels, and insurgents, their aiders and abettors" were subjected to martial law and trial by military commission, and further, suspended the writ of habeas corpus for all persons, "...confined by military authority."[13]

Up to this point the suspension of the writ had been supported by presidential authority only in narrowly defined cases. This new proclamation, however, had broad and sweeping implications. The suspension pertained only to those instances which involved military arrest of civilians presumably based on military necessity. While this suspension of the writ had a very precise applicability, it became an order for wholesale arrests.

The use of military commissions throughout the war was not in any way infrequent. During the four-year period approximately two thousand commissions sat in judgment over nearly thirteen thousand defendants and were not at all adverse to "harsh judgments."[14]

This relatively new form of justice actually had its origins during the war with Mexico in 1846. When General Winfield Scott took his American forces into Mexico he was faced with a dilemma which the American military had never before encountered. He was forced to improvise ways to deal with serious crimes committed by civilians within his military area which would have been triable in the civil courts in the United States. Not having such courts available to try American citizens for their alleged offenses while in Mexico, Scott established two courts on his own: the military commission, which handled civil offenses, and the council of war, which covered offenses against the "laws of war." Scott took these actions reluctantly and only after unsuccessfully petitioning the Congress of the United States for direction in this troublesome matter.

Scott's council of war did not survive the Mexican conflict, and was merged into the military commission which also assumed the responsibility for trying those cases involving offenses against the "laws of war."

It is interesting to note that the authority for military commissions throughout this period was without statutory basis. Their legal basis and utilization were never directly challenged before the Supreme Court during the four years of the Civil War save in one peculiar instance. In this one case where the Supreme Court had an opportunity to hear and rule on the legal jurisdiction of the military tribunal, it effectively avoided the issue by declaring that it lacked jurisdiction.

The case involved Ohio congressman Clement L. Vallandigham, a notorious Copperhead.[15] Vallandigham had been arrested by the military for his "anti-war" efforts in Ohio and elsewhere. He was brought to trial before a military tribunal in Cincinnati in 1863. Found guilty, he was ordered banished from Union soil to a point within the military lines of the Confederacy. Vallandigham filed a petition with the Supreme Court for a writ of habeas corpus and challenged the legal jurisdiction of the military tribunal that tried him.[16] Just two years after Chief Justice Taney had challenged Lincoln, the Court effectively sidestepped the tricky issue by ruling that it was without jurisdiction in the case, the military commission falling outside the Judicial Act of 1789. In so doing, the Court, in effect, gave its back-of-the-hand approval to the military commission as a war court. Interestingly, in the several cases which have come before the Supreme Court over the eighty-three year period involving military commissions, the court has never ruled against the authority of the military commission, only to its jurisdiction in specified instances.

The use of the military commission was put to its severest test following the assassination of Lincoln. With all but two of the charged conspirators in shackles, the new president, Andrew Johnson, issued an Executive Order on May 1, 1865, subjecting those charged with the former president's murder to stand trial before a military commission composed of nine Union officers.[17]

While the reasons for turning to a military trial may be varied, as has been speculated, we have only the written justifications of the principal jurist to guide us. Attorney General James Speed issued an official opinion on the legal jurisdiction of the tribunal as ordered by President Johnson.[18]

Speed's lengthy opinion, often rambling far afield, seems at times to attempt to legitimize the commission by sheer weight of words. Its essence, however, reduces down to two important and substantive points: that the offenses which the accused were charged with were offenses against the laws of war, and that the defendants were, in fact, "belligerents" who served as, "...secret, but active participants (spies) in the recent hostilities."[19] Thus Speed cast a net about the hapless accused which placed them in an exclusionary category, and denied them trial in the civil courts which lacked jurisdiction over such offenses and persons. The Supreme Court had already supported this notion in the Vallandigham case.[20]

In his opinion Speed asserts that, "If the question be one concerning the laws of war, he (the accused) should be tried by those engaged in the war— they and only they are his peers. The military must decide whether the accused is or is not a participant in the hostilities. If he is an active participant in the hostilities, it is the duty of the military to take him prisoner without warrant or other judicial process, and dispose of him as the laws of war direct."[21] This point which Speed effectively develops in his opinion to Johnson is not dismissed lightly. Some historians express the view that a certain hysteria of the times equated participation in the rebellion with participation in the assassination. While this position may have some basis in fact, it should not cloud or confuse Speed's conclusion that the accused conspirators were Confederate agents (belligerents) and therefore legally triable before a military tribunal. The distinction is important.

Despite the feeling by some that the attorney general was not guided by constitutional law in developing his opinion regarding the jurisdiction of the military tribunal, Speed was quite cognizant of the constitutional provisions which later came to haunt the commission and its advocates. In his opinion, Speed acknowledges the existence of the civil courts in the District of Columbia and their jurisdiction under normal circumstances, but dismisses their right to try the accused conspirators, writing,

> The fact that the civil courts are open does not affect the right of the military tribunal to hold (the accused) as a prisoner and to try. The civil courts have no more right to prevent the military, **in time of war**, from trying **offenders against the laws of war** than they have a right to interfere with and prevent a battle.[22]

It was the government's contention that the commander-in-chief of the armed forces had been murdered by enemy agents within a military zone which had been subjected to an invasion attempt by hostile forces at a time when martial law existed.[23] It further asserted that martial law supersedes civil law in every instance. The defense countered by challenging the legality of the military commission as a court in what should have been a strictly civil matter. The accused were civilians (not enemy belligerents) charged with what should be a civil offense, conspiracy to murder, and therefore should be tried in the civil courts of the District of Columbia which were open and functioning without difficulty. The defense further maintained that the need or justification for martial law ended with the surrender of Lee on April 9, 1865.

Not unexpectedly, the military commission ruled that the challenge to its legal justification was without merit and the trial proceeded over the continued protests of the defense. The question of the military commission's jurisdiction arose again, not just once, but several times over the next eighty years. The first hard test arose scarcely a year after the 1865 conspiracy trial in a case soon to become famous known as *ex parte Milligan*.[24]

Lambdin P. Milligan, a long-time resident of Indiana and a citizen of the United States, had been actively engaged in a series of overt acts in opposition to the federal government's prosecution of the war, playing a major role in organizing a chapter of the Order of the Sons of Liberty in 1863 within the state of Indiana. This group had as one of its objectives the forced take-over of certain government arsenals in the Midwest, together with the attempted liberation of thousands of Confederate prisoners of war from various Northern camps. This elaborate scheme by Milligan and his collaborators was no amateurish operation, and disastrous consequences of this internal threat to Union efforts were quickly recognized. Federal agents had successfully infiltrated Milligan's organization and closely monitored its activity. In May 1864, Major General Alvin P. Hovey, who commanded the military district encompassing Indiana, ordered the arrest of Milligan and several of his supporters.[25] Milligan was tried before a military commission in Indianapolis, found guilty on all counts and was sentenced to death by hanging.

Milligan, an accomplished lawyer who had been admitted to the bar with another accomplished lawyer, Edwin M. Stanton, immediately petitioned the United States Circuit Court for Indiana on a writ of habeas corpus following his conviction. Milligan's plea was based on his belief that he had been tried and sentenced by a military commission which lacked legal jurisdiction.

The court that received Milligan's petition consisted of Judge David McDonald and Supreme Court Justice David Davis who was sitting as a circuit court judge during the Supreme Court recess. Davis was strongly opposed to the death penalty and to the use of military commissions to try civilians during wartime, and these feelings were well known by those familiar with his career.

Davis felt that the military holding Milligan would ignore the circuit court ruling and would proceed to execute him under "Presidential authority." Davis shrewdly persuaded Judge McDonald to "oppose" him in their ruling to take advantage of a procedure whereby if two judges of a circuit court are divided on a question of law, they could take the question to the Supreme Court for an answer. Davis then convinced President Johnson to commute Milligan's death sentence to life imprisonment, thereby allowing a resolution of the issue before the Supreme Court which would not have been possible if Milligan had been executed.[26]

On March 6, 1866, the petition came before the Supreme Court in its spring session. Three questions were posed to the court on which Davis and McDonald claimed they were opposed:

1. *On the facts stated in said petition and exhibits, ought the writ of habeas corpus to be issued?*
2. *On the facts stated in said petition and exhibits, ought the said Lambdin P. Milligan to be discharged from custody as in said petition prayed?*
3. *Whether upon the facts stated in said petition and exhibits, the military commission mentioned therein had jurisdiction legally to try and sentence said Milligan in manner and form in said petition and exhibits stated?*

The justices listened to the two groups of advocates as they pressed their cases. The government position was argued by Henry Stanberry (soon to become Andrew Johnson's attorney general), Benjamin F. Butler and Attorney General James F. Speed. The thrust of their argument lay in the authority of the president of the United States to order certain persons charged with offenses against the laws of war tried before a military commission in those areas where martial law was in effect.

Representing Milligan were a group of distinguished Americans whose credentials were impressive. Opening the defense was James A. Garfield, future president and only admitted to practice before the court that very morning. Garfield was accompanied by J. E. McDonald who had defeated Milligan for the Democratic nomination for governor of Indiana the previous year only to lose to Oliver P. Morton, the man who persuaded President Johnson to commute Milligan's sentence. Rounding the quartet of defense attorneys was the prominent jurist, Jeremiah S. Black, former attorney general under Buchanan and currently a judge of the Pennsylvania Supreme Court, and David Dudley Field, the brother of sitting Supreme Court Justice Stephen S. Field.

The defense argued simply, if somewhat excessively, that Milligan was not, nor ever had been in the military service of the United States, that the civil courts in Indiana were open and functioning freely, and that constitutional guarantees of a civil trial by a jury of his peers had been denied him.

The importance of the Milligan case centered around three key points dealing with: the privilege of the writ of habeas corpus which had been denied to Milligan, the existence of martial law, and the constitutional guarantees concerning the preeminence of civil courts in time of peace and war.

The court ruling has since been hailed as a landmark decision in American jurisprudence and one of a dozen cases considered to be the foundation of American civil liberties. The court ruled unanimously that the only authority under which a military commission could exist was that derived from the "laws and usages of war," but that the laws of war can never apply to citizens in jurisdictions where the civil courts were open and functioning, and that the president has no authority, constitutional or otherwise, to order anyone to stand trial before a military commission under the circumstances described in Milligan's case.[27]

The prosecution's contention that the military commission was justified under the rule of martial law resulting from Lincoln's Proclamation of 1862 was held invalid. The court said that martial law can only apply in the case of actual invasion or civil war where the courts are closed and it is impossible to administer justice except by the power of the military. Martial law, therefore, was limited to the zone of actual combat, and not to an area where only the threat of invasion existed.

On the question of habeas corpus, the court neither affirmed nor denied the president's authority to suspend the writ saying, "Unquestionably there is an urgency which demands that the government should not be required to produce the persons arrested in answer to a writ of habeas corpus." But who is the government? The president or the Congress, or both?[28]

If the court still left that issue somewhat clouded, it did affirm that Congress in its Act of March 21, 1863, specified the conditions and circumstances associated with the suspension of the writ. Prisoners were not to be kept confined indefinitely, but their cases were to be presented to a grand jury at the next regular session. In the absence of an indictment by the grand jury, they were to be released immediately. If indicted, they would be tried in a civil court by a jury of their peers as guaranteed by the Sixth Amendment of the Constitution. Thus, while a person may be denied the privilege of having his jailers present him before a civil court to determine whether and on what grounds he should continue to be held, he must be taken before a grand jury and indicted or set free. This procedure was a far cry from what in fact was taking place throughout the North during the war; and it was this very practice that formed the basis for Milligan's plea.

Many historians have applied a broad brush to the Supreme Court's ruling in Milligan concluding that the court declared military commissions illegal in those areas where the civil courts were open and functioning. This is incorrect. Such a conclusion is an oversimplification and does not reflect the court's complete ruling. The decision was not so sweeping in its meaning and Justice David Davis, the man directly responsible for the Milligan case coming before the court, said as much in a letter which he later wrote discussing the decision. Davis maintained that the decision applied only to the trial of civilians in certain parts of the North during the war.[29]

It is important to understand that the Supreme Court did not rule that military commissions were illegal, only that their jurisdiction was carefully limited to certain conditions which must be met. The court felt that none of the requisite conditions existed in Indiana or applied to Milligan which would make him subject to military authority.

Certainly the Milligan case casts an ominous shadow over the Lincoln conspiracy trial, leading many students of this episode to declare it illegal. Among them were the lawyers of Dr. Mudd. Quickly following on the heels of the Milligan decision was a petition filed with the Supreme Court on behalf of Dr. Mudd and his cohorts. Mudd, Edman Spangler and Samuel B. Arnold were languishing off the Florida Keys in the federal prison at Dry Tortugas when the Milligan decision was released. The defendants claimed that *ex parte Milligan* applied equally to their case and that the military tribunal which had tried them (and hanged Mary Surratt, Lewis Powell, Davy Herold and George Atzerodt) was illegal.

On December 29, 1866, Chief Justice Salmon P. Chase reviewed the petition and returned it stating that, "...the petition should be addressed to a Court or Judge of the United States in the District within which the prisoner is held."[30] In August 1868, Mudd's lawyers followed Chief Justice Chase's direction and made application for a writ of habeas corpus to the United States District Court for the Southern District of Florida.

Hearing their petition was Judge Thomas Jefferson Boynton who presided over the District Court of the United States for the Southern District of Florida. Mudd's petition to Boynton went beyond citing *ex parte Milligan* by stating that, "...if the military commission was legal in their case," then President Johnson's proclamation of July 4, 1867, granting general amnesty to all persons associated with the rebellion applied equally to them.

Boynton, however, ruled against the petition denying its validity on both points.[31] The judge wrote that the Milligan decision did not apply to the Lincoln conspirators, and that Johnson's amnesty proclamation specifically excluded all persons being held in military prisons, and "...all persons who were engaged directly or indirectly in the assassination of the late President...or in any plot or conspiracy in any manner therein connected."

Boynton maintained that a sharp difference existed between the cases of Milligan and Mudd. Indiana was not in a military situation; that is, it had not been invaded and did not have a hostile army camped within or adjacent to its borders. In sum, it was not an active zone of combat, and the crime which Milligan was accused of was not against the laws of war. In contrast, Boynton considered Washington an active zone of combat and its commander-in-chief murdered, not from private malice, but as a military necessity to effect military and political objectives. Boynton wrote:

> *The president was assassinated not from private animosity nor any other reason than a desire to impair the effectiveness of military operations, and enable the rebellion to establish itself into a Government; the act was committed in a fortified city, which had been invaded during the war, and to the northward as well as the southward of which battles had many times been fought, which was the headquarters of all the armies of the United States, from which daily and hourly went military orders. The President is the Commander-in-Chief of the army, and the President who was killed had many times made distinct military orders under his own hand, without the formality of employing the name of the Secretary of War or Commanding-General. It was not Mr. Lincoln who was assassinated, but the Commander-in-Chief, for military reasons. I find no difficulty, therefore, in classing the offense as a military one, and with this opinion, arrive at the necessary conclusion that the proper tribunal for the trial of those engaged was a military one.[32]*

Strongly reminiscent of Speed's opinion two years earlier, Boynton finessed around the principal argument arising from the Milligan decision by placing the accused in an exclusionary category. Mudd and his compatriots were cast in a net they could not wriggle out of.

Mudd was not finished just yet, however. His lawyers were now prepared to take Boynton's denial to the Supreme Court. As the petition was being prepared, President Johnson issued his pardon of Dr. Mudd on February 8, 1869. Deleting Mudd from the petition, the application was filed with the court on behalf of Samuel Arnold and Edman Spangler on February 19, 1869. Being petitions for habeas corpus, they were expedited and arguments were heard on February 26, 1869. Before the court issued an opinion, however, President Johnson followed his pardon of Dr. Mudd by issuing pardons for Arnold and Spangler rendering a decision by the court moot. The petitions were dismissed on March 19, leaving all of the arguments in place with no decision. Regardless of the arguments for or against the military tribunal and Mudd's personal situation within the American justice system, he clearly had his day in court and was not denied post-trial due process.

If the Supreme Court had put to rest the question of jurisdiction of military tribunals with its decision in *ex parte Milligan* as many historians have concluded, its ruling was as gossamer as was the decision in Dred Scott. Immediately following the cessation of hostilities and the death of Lincoln, the radicals of Lincoln's party began sweeping through the

Southland with a vengeful force. The period of Reconstruction saw an expansive use of the military tribunal enforcing a policy of retribution against the defeated rebels. As the Northern victors established control throughout the Southern states, they solidified their power through military justice. Despite *ex parte Milligan* (which raised the Radicals wrath toward the Supreme Court to an unprecedented level), the military commission lived on in apparent disregard for the court's ruling. It should be remembered that the court in its Milligan ruling not only reaffirmed the jurisdiction of the civil courts where they were open and functioning, but narrowly defined the circumstances under which martial law could legally exist as it did throughout the reconstructed South.

Close on the heels of the Milligan decision, Johnson ordered a cessation to all military trials involving civilians. The Radicals, more determined than ever to carry out their purification program, maneuvered around Johnson and his "obstructionist" Supreme Court with the passage of the Reconstruction Act of March 2, 1867. The Act created five military districts in eleven southern states (Tennessee was excluded) and placed each under the command of a Union general.[33] Each district was subject to martial law, and the military tribunal continued to operate in defiance of *ex parte Milligan* under the protective umbrella of the Reconstruction Act.

Both President Johnson and certain members of the Supreme Court indicated their feelings that the act was unconstitutional. The radicals continued to live with a growing fear that their policies would eventually be blocked by these two adversaries. Soon after the Milligan ruling the court found itself embroiled in still another controversy which generated great heat. Two cases had come before the court involving test-oaths which required certain individuals to attest to their loyalty to the United States and to their never having served or aided the recently defeated Confederacy in any manner. The court, in a close five to four vote, held that the loyalty oaths were unconstitutional in that they imposed a punishment ex post facto.[34] Once again the radical members of Congress leveled their fury at the court and its "undoing" of all they were accomplishing. As the storm swirled about the heads of the justices, a third "reconstruction" case came before the already bruised bench which had the Radicals snarling even more viciously than before.

William C. McCardle, an ex-Confederate colonel and the editor of a Vicksburg newspaper, had been arrested and held for trial before a military tribunal. McCardle had been charged with the dual crimes of insulting Major General E. O. C. Ord and of strongly opposing the Reconstruction Acts in his newspaper's editorials. Upon his arrest, McCardle applied to the federal court for release on a writ of habeas corpus. The court denied McCardle's petition, and he promptly petitioned the Supreme Court for relief.[35]

The Radical members of Congress, now more sure than ever that the court would again rule on the wrong side of Reconstruction, quickly moved to block any further meddling by the justices. After the case had been presented and before the justices had convened to issue their opinion, both houses of Congress, in a single day, passed an act which selectively removed the court's appellate jurisdiction under the Act of February, 1867. When the court finally did convene, it had no other recourse but to dismiss the petition on the grounds that the Supreme Court lacked jurisdiction in the case, thus sending McCardle back to his military captors.[36] And so the rule of martial law throughout the South continued to be administered by the military through their tribunals in spite of Milligan.

For the next seven and a half decades the question of military tribunals lay in obscurity, all but disappearing from the American scene. It would probably have remained so if it had not been for its resurrection during the Second World War. The interval between the Civil War and World War II saw no circumstances in which military tribunals held court. Then, during the summer of 1942, eight German agents secretly landed along the coast of the United States; four on Long Island, New York, and four along the coast of Florida. Within two weeks all eight would-be saboteurs had been arrested by the FBI, and were brought to Washington, D. C.[37]

President Franklin Delano Roosevelt quickly issued a Presidential Proclamation calling for the establishment of a military tribunal, and at the same time denying the accused access to the civil courts.[38] Roosevelt's proclamation was strikingly reminiscent of Andrew Johnson's proclamation issued nearly eighty years earlier.

The defense attorneys for the eight prisoners petitioned the Supreme Court on a writ of habeas corpus and challenged the jurisdiction of a military tribunal citing *ex parte Milligan* as their defense. As in 1865, the climate was clearly against the defendants and any claim of civil liberties which they might present. The nation was engaged in a war which could clearly end in defeat, for the summer of 1942 was not a time of optimism for America and her military.

The Supreme Court, already in summer recess, startled the entire world by agreeing to reconvene in an emergency session to hear the defendants' petition. Here indeed was a headline event. Perhaps the court wanted to show the world, and especially totalitarian nations, America's great concern for civil liberties—even for those who would destroy the very Constitution they now sought to wrap around themselves.

The circumstances surrounding *ex parte Quirin* were similar in many ways to those associated with Milligan and with the Lincoln conspirators a century before. The United States was part of a military zone which had been penetrated by enemy belligerents. The accused were charged with offenses against the laws of war, and the president, by executive order, had made them subject to martial law thus denying a trial by jury in the civil courts. All this had been claimed by the government in 1865 and again in 1942.

The defense in citing *ex parte Milligan* pointed out to the court that the civil courts were open and functioning, that no invasion or threat of invasion was imminent, and that the civil authority was not compelled to operate with the support of bayonets.

In its ruling[39] the court took a turn which should seem curious to students of *ex parte Milligan*. The court held that the president had authority to create a military commission, and that indictment by a grand jury and a trial by jury were not applicable—the defendants were charged with "offenses against the laws of war." The ruling in 1942, more than any other, is strongly reminiscent of Attorney General James Speed's opinion of July 1865 in regard to the Lincoln conspirators.

So Quirin and his collaborators went on trial before a military commission and were found guilty and sentenced—all with the sanction of the Supreme Court.[40]

The Supreme Court's affair with the military commission did not end here, however. By the summer of 1945 the Allied Armies had reversed the dark days of 1942 and had rolled to total victory over the Axis Powers. With the final surrender of the Japanese forces in the Philippines, the military was once again challenged before the Supreme Court in its efforts to use the military tribunal as a final court of justice.

With the fall of the Philippines early in 1945, Japanese General Tomoyuki Yamashita, the "Tiger of Malaya," surrendered his Imperial Japanese 14th Army Group and became a prisoner of war. United States military authorities decided to charge Yamashita with responsibility for all of the atrocities committed by the soldiers under his command in the closing weeks of the war. While U. S. authorities acknowledged that Yamashita never ordered or condoned (or was even aware of) the atrocities being committed, he was nevertheless held responsible for all of their actions.

Once again the Supreme Court was asked to decide on the jurisdiction of a military tribunal in trying defendants when the civil courts were open and functioning, and once again, Milligan became the defense.[41]

While Yamashita was a military officer and an enemy belligerent, his crimes were crimes against civilians triable in the civil courts in the jurisdiction where the alleged offenses occurred. While there may seem to be little in common between Yamashita and the conspiracy trial of 1865, the questions answered by the Supreme Court in Yamashita have direct bearing on our consideration of the legal jurisdiction of the Lincoln conspiracy trial in 1865.

Eighty years after its ruling in *ex parte Milligan*, the Supreme Court went against its ruling of 1866 and said that the Congress of the United States had the authority to establish military commissions and that its authority was derived directly from the Constitution under Article I, paragraph 8, which states in part that Congress could "...define and punish...offenses against the Law of nations...," a principal clause cited by Speed in 1865 in support of his opinion to President Johnson. This latter decision, eighty years after Milligan, seems in sharp contrast to the court's original decision. The court went on to state that the authority of the military tribunal rested in the charge that the defendant was accused of "violations against the laws of war," and therefore should be tried before a military tribunal.

> *Neither congressional action nor military orders constituting the commission authorized it to place the petitioner on trial unless the charge preferred against him is a violation of the laws of war. We conclude that the allegations of the charge, tested by any reasonable standard, adequately allege a violation of the law of war and that the military commission has authority to try and decide the issue which it raised.*

As in the case of the Lincoln conspirators, Yamashita's trial took place after all hostilities had ceased. The Supreme Court pointed out in their ruling, however, that the **cessation of hostilities does not end the jurisdiction of the military commission.** This point is important to the issue of the Lincoln trial. Critics of the Lincoln conspiracy trial have claimed that the surrender of Lee's army ended all threat of military invasion and thereby eliminated the jurisdiction of the military court. Like Quirin, et. Al., Yamashita faced the military tribunal, was found guilty and was executed with the full sanction of the Supreme Court.

In these two modern wartime rulings the Supreme Court clearly defined the defendants as enemy belligerents who were rightfully charged with committing offenses against the laws of war and therefore fell under the jurisdiction of the military tribunal.

Reviewing the judicial record with respect to military tribunals over a period of eighty years, what conclusions may be drawn with reference to the case of the Lincoln conspirators? In its most famous case, *ex parte Milligan,* the Supreme Court clearly defined the circumstances in which martial law may legally exist.[42]

The court did not rule, as some claim, that military commissions were without jurisdiction where the civil courts were open and functioning. The military commission clearly had jurisdiction in those cases in which offenses against the laws of war were charged, and the Supreme Court sanctioned such authority on several occasions. The court made this clear in Milligan, and in Quirin and in Yamashita. The court went further in stating in Milligan that he was not an enemy belligerent and that he was not charged with offenses against the laws of war.

If we interpret the court's ruling in Milligan as only acknowledging the jurisdiction of military commissions in those circumstances in which the civil courts are closed and unable to administer justice, then it went against itself in Vallandigham, Quirin and Yamashita—all cases involving military tribunals in areas in which the civil courts were open and were carrying on their business unimpeded.

When, then, are military tribunals legal? They are legal in those cases where martial law exists and the civil courts are forced to close, or when the accused are enemy belligerents charged with violations of the laws of war. Quirin and Yamashita were defined as enemy belligerents charged with offenses against the laws of war. In Yamashita, the court ruled that persons charged with violations against the laws of war were rightfully tried by a military commission. In Quirin, the court ruled that the president of the United States has the authority to establish military commissions and that persons who are accused as belligerents or secret agents (spies) are subject to trial before such commissions.

How are these cases applicable to our understanding of the Lincoln conspiracy trial? The government's justification for a military trial was premised on the fact that the accused conspirators were, in fact, belligerents who were agents and sympathizers of the rebellion who operated in stealth and in concert.

In his opinion of July 1865, Attorney General James Speed developed the position that the defendants were enemy belligerents who conspired to murder the commander-in-chief behind military lines within an active war zone and thus committed offenses against the laws of war. They were not civilians or entitled to be considered as civilians. The original conspiracy was designed to capture the commander-in-chief of United States forces, a military offense. The accused having met the test as enemy belligerents, the president had the authority to establish the military commission before which they were tried.

The key factor, it seems, is not in the kind of court that administers justice, but in the alleged offense and the nature of the offender. Having decided these two questions, the proper jurisdiction (court) follows.

Certainly sufficient evidence exists which shows that Booth, Surratt, Atzerodt, and Mudd all performed services for the Confederacy as agents in moving supplies or people across military lines. Powell, O'Laughlen, and Arnold served in the Confederate army.[43] Only Mary Surratt, Herold, and Spangler are without any known ties to the Confederate Secret Service or military although many believe that since the two Surratt houses served as safe houses for Confederate agents it was not without Mary Surratt's knowledge and participation.

From the cases reviewed, it appears that the mood of the court is influenced by the state of the nation at the time of ruling. During wartime, the court favors a military position; during peacetime, the court favors a civil position.

Had the court issued an opinion on the petition of Arnold and Spangler in 1869, it appears likely that their decision would have been in favor of the legal jurisdiction of the military commission consistent with the court's later rulings in the twentieth century.

Judge Boynton made a clear distinction between Indiana and the District of Columbia in ruling on Mudd's petition before the District Court in Florida. That distinction comes through in the court's subsequent rulings during and shortly after World War Two.

While the question of Dr. Mudd's guilt or innocence is entirely separate from the legal jurisdiction of his trial, the historical evidence supports the legality of the military commission to try Mudd and his co-defendants.

Admittedly, the history of the military commission is sordid, but it nevertheless occupies an important place in American jurisprudence. The question of whether Dr. Mudd was legally tried and convicted, like so many other controversial incidents of the Civil War, must forever remain an arguable subject. One fact is clear, however, whatever history thinks of the military tribunal and its jurisdiction: Dr. Mudd was allowed every avenue of access to the American justice system, both before the U. S. District Court (Southern District of Florida) and before the Supreme Court of the United States.

While Mudd's proponents may be unhappy with the decisions rendered by the judicial system, they cannot claim that Mudd was denied due process following his conviction. The good doctor had his day in court, both military and civil, and despite the concerted efforts and good intentions of his defenders—his name is still Mudd.

APPENDIX

1

I reside in Charles County, Maryland, near Bryantown, about 25 miles from Washington. My house is, I suppose, between 18 & 20 miles from the nearest point on the Potomac river, and about 60 or 70 miles from the west shore of the Chesapeake. I am a physician by profession, and have been practicing some 9 years, having graduated in 1856 in Baltimore.

I first heard of the assassination of President Lincoln on Saturday afternoon (April 15) about two or three o'clock in the afternoon.

There are two or three physicians besides myself living in that immediate neighborhood. The village in which I live is a very small one, having only some 8 or 10 houses in it.

About 4 o'clock on Saturday morning, the 15th, two persons came to my house and commenced rapping very loudly at the door. I was very much alarmed at this, fearing it might be somebody who had come there not for any good purpose, and hesitated at first about going down. On their knocking very heavily the second time, I aroused my wife, and we conferred with one another a moment as to who should go to the door. She thought she had better go as it might be some one who came there with an evil intent. Knowing her nervous nature, however, I determined it would be better for me to go. I, therefore, concluded to do so. Before opening the door, however, I inquired who was there. They told me two strangers from St. Marys Co. who were on their way to Washington; but that the horse of one of them had fallen, and broken the rider's leg. Satisfying myself of the correctness of the statement of one of them having received an injury, by going to a window & seeing one of them in distress, I went and opened the door.

I took them into the parlor, and laid the injured man on the sofa, until I could get a light, when I took him upstairs. His friend urged me to attend to his leg as soon as possible, as they were very anxious to get to Washington ; and then it is my impression he enquired (sic) if they could not reach some point on the Potomac where they could get a boat to Washington.

I examined the injured leg, but did not give it a very thorough examination owing to the parties wanting it attended to in such haste. My examination was sufficiently thorough, however, to enable me to discover that there was one bone broken about two inches above the ankle joint—what we call a "direct fracture." In setting the limb, having no splinters, or anything of that sort at hand, I was compelled to cut up an old band-box and use it. I do not remember of their having assigned any reason for their great haste— other than that they had made an early start and were anxious to get to Washington as soon as possible.

As regard the personal appearance of these two men, one was a very small one. I should call him a well grown boy. He looked to be about 17 or 18—to be a boy who had never yet shaved. The other was a man of medium size, with black hair. He had whiskers, and also a moustache.

A photograph of Booth was afterwards shown me by a detective, but I did not observe any resemblance between the two men, though I must say that I have very often been shown likenesses of intimate friends, and failed to recognize them by their pictures. The last man I have described had a black streak down the side of his face.

These men remained at my house until 4 & 5 o'clock in the afternoon. I never saw either of the parties before, nor can I conceive who sent them to my house. They themselves gave me no intimation on the subject.

The man whose leg was broken had on a dark suit but I cannot tell whether he had on pants, coat & vest of the same material and color, or not. The injured man had very little to say. He had a heavy shawl which he kept around him; and he seemed to be laboring under considerable nervousness, or pain.

I was at home pretty much all day, and was in the room where they were at short intervals. The reason I took them upstairs was because I had no room downstairs. Including the entry recently built between the house and the kitchen, and the kitchen itself, there are five rooms on the lower floor, which is occupied by myself and wife.

I had very little conversation with these men during the day, though one (the smaller) seemed to be quite communicative, and well acquainted through out the whole neighborhood. Nothing was said by them leading me to infer that they had been engaged in any such deed as this assassination.

The small one also had on a dark suit, with black hair.

After the injured man had got off of his horse, the other one asked me if I could not have the two horses stabled, as one of them would not suffer herself to be hitched. I went after the boy, and he held them until the boy came.

I did not see the parties when they left in the afternoon. The small one said he would not need any one to assist him in putting the injured man on the horse as he had before put him on at the time he broke his leg; so I did not go out.

My family at this time consisted of my wife, four children, a widow lady, and a sister-in-law. There are three working hands on the place—two white and one colored. I think my wife saw them for a short time after dinner, when she went up to know whether they would have anything more, or desired any particular diet. I do not think any others of the family saw them.

They requested me to have a pair of crutches made after I set the leg when I got two arm pieces and whittled them out as best I could. I afterwards gave them to the old man who works on the farm to put a stick in.

They paid me $25 for my services, which they rather pressed me to accept. I told them a small fee would answer.

Before they left they inquired the way to the Rev. Wilmer's, an acquaintance of mine, who resides not far from Beantown. His house is about five miles from mine, round the road, and about 4 directly across. I think they took the road across as they inquired for the nearest road. He is regarded by neighbors as a Union man. I have always called myself a Union man, though I have never voted with the administration party. I have never heard any expression from my neighbors as to what they thought of me in that respect.

I do not think any of my neighbors saw these men at my house. I think I first communicated the fact of these men stopping at my house under these circumstances to Mr. John F. Hardy, and Frances Farrell. It was on Saturday evening when I did so if my memory serves me right.

This injured man had boots on, but whether he had spurs on or not I dismember. I had to cut the boot from the injured limb. This boot he left, and it is now in possession of the military authorities.

The names given by these parties—the young man Henson, and the other Tyson or Tyser. There are some Hansons down in our neighborhood who are regularly called Hensons.

I only saw one of these horses. That one was a small bay mare, with a natural tail as far as I could observe. I did not notice any white scars, or spots about him. This horse was a very lively one.

The older of these men I should judge to be about 30 or 35 years of age.

I first heard of the assassination of President Lincoln at Bryantown.

The injured man after having his leg set seemed to suffer a good deal of pain, and said he did not think he would be able to travel on horseback, and desired to get a carriage, buggy, or something of the sort that he might be enabled to continue his journey. I told him I had nothing of the sort, but that perhaps, he might get an old carriage from my father, and that as I was going to ride out that afternoon, the young man might go over there with me, and see if he could do so. After dinner, the young man ordered the bay mare, and then we rode over to my father's together. We found my father out, but saw my brother who was getting his horse ready to go to the Post Office, or to church. I asked him if he could lend a carriage. He said the carriage he had was old & very much out of repair, and unfit to travel in, any distance. While I was holding this conversation with my brother this young man stood just behind a house in front of the shed where I was engaged in talking.

My brother not being willing to take the responsibility of lending this carriage, the young man said he would go to Bryantown, and endeavor to get a conveyance there. He started off at a pretty fair gallop and I after him. He soon got a good distance ahead of me as his horse was quite a sprightly one, while mine was a very dull one. When he got a mile and a half beyond my father's house, he abruptly turned round and came back, meeting me as he did so. He seemed to be engaged in deep thought. As he passed me he observed, "I believe I will get my friend to go to Rev. Dr. Wilmer's on horseback." He, therefore, did not go to Bryantown—at least with me. My object in going there was to purchase some articles which were needed by the family; and I thought I would at the same time see about some nails that were intended for immediate use. I purchased at Mr. Beans some calico & some pepper, for which I paid him. I got back to the house between 4 & 5 o'clock. The two men were just getting ready to start when I got back. It was about 12 o'clock when we had dinner. One of the men, the young one, ate dinner with me. The other one had his dinner sent to him.

I was not where I could see these men mount their horses at the time of their departure. I was down at the front of my place below the swamp. In describing the way to Rev. Wilmer's I told them that in going across this swamp there would be but one fence to pull down between that place and the barn, which would lead them to the place where they desired to go.

No suspicion was aroused in my mind of anything being wrong with regard to these men. After I had heard of the assassination, and began to have suspicion as to these two men being in some way connected with it, a little circumstance occurred to me as confirmatory of such suspicions & which I had not thought of before. It was this. After breakfast the older one asked for a razor and some soap; which he got; and on my giving him the articles which I had prepared, a short time afterward, I noticed that his moustache had disappeared.

The pantaloons of this man were covered with mud in many places; and the appearance of his clothes would in other respects indicate that he had been riding very rapidly.

I mentioned my suspicion of these men, and the circumstance of the moustache being removed, the next morning to a "brother" physician, a relative of mine, Dr. Geo. Mudd and I think also to Mr. Wm. Mudd and Mr. T. L. Gardiner.

The injured man had a belt with two revolvers in it concealed under his clothing, which I discovered when he got into bed after having his wound dressed. I did not discover whether the other one was armed or not.

Appendix

$$2$$

Statement of Dr. S. A. Mudd
In the matter of the murder of the President
April 21, 1865
Bryantown, Md. April 21, 1865

Dr. S. A. Mudd, residing 4 miles north of Bryantown, Maryland, being duly sworn deposes and says:

Last Saturday morning, April 15th, about four o'clock, two men called at my house and knocked very loudly. I was aroused by the noise, and as it was such an unusual thing for persons to knock so loudly, I took the precaution of asking who were there before opening the door. After they had knocked twice more, I opened the door, but before doing so they told me they were two strangers on their way to Washington, that one of their horses had fallen by which one of the men had broken his leg. On opening the door, I found two men, one on a horse led by the other man who had tied his horse to a tree near by. I aided the man in getting off of his horse and into the house, and laid him on a sofa in my parlor. After getting a light, I assisted him in getting upstairs where there were two beds, one of which he took. He seemed to be very much injured in the back, and complained very much of it. I did not see his face at all. He seemed to be tremulous and not inclined to talk, and had his cloak thrown around his head and seemed inclined to sleep, as I thought in order to ease himself, and every now and then he would groan pretty heavily. I had no proper paste-board for making splints, and went and got an old band-box and made one of it; and as he wanted it done hastily, I hurried more than I otherwise would. He wanted me to fix it up anyway, as he said he wanted to get back, or get home and have it done by a regular physician. I then took a piece of the band-box and split it in half, doubled it at right angles, and took some past (sic) and pasted it into a splint. On examination, I found there was a straight fracture of the tibia about two inches above the ankle. My examination was quite short, and I did not find the adjoining bone fractured in any way. I do not regard it a peculiarly painful or dangerous wound; there was nothing resembling a compound fracture. I do not suppose I was more than three-quarters of an hour in making the examination of the wound and applying the splint. He continued still to suffer, and complained of severe pain in the back, especially when being moved. In my opinion, pain in the back may originate from riding; I judge that in this case it originated from his fall and also from riding, as he seemed to be prostrated. He sometimes breathed very shortly and as if exhausted. He was a man, I should suppose about five feet ten inches high, and appeared to be pretty well made, but he had a heavy shawl on all the time. I suppose he would weigh 150 or 160 pounds. His hair was black and seemed to be somewhat inclined to curl; it was long. He had a pretty full forehead and his skin was fair. He was very pale when I saw him, and appeared as if accustomed to in-door rather than out-door life. I do not know how to describe his skin exactly but I should think he might be classed as dark, and his paleness might be attributed to receiving the injury. I did not observe his hand to see if it was small or large. I have been shown the photograph of J. Wilkes Booth and I should not think that this was the man from any resemblance to the photograph, but from other causes I have every reason to believe that he is the man whose leg I dressed as above stated.

In order to examine and operate upon his leg, I had occasion to cut his boot longitudinally in front of the instep. It seems that when he left my house, this boot was left behind. Yesterday morning my attention was called to this boot which is a long and top-boot. On making an examination of it, I find written on the inside in apparently a German hand, what I take to be "Henry Luz, maker 445 Broadway, J. Wilkes." I did not notice the writing in this boot until my attention was called to it by Lieutenant Lovett. (Boot produced and identified by deponent as the one taken from the leg of the wounded man.)

I have seen J. Wilkes Booth. I was introduced to him by Mr. J. C. Thompson, a son-in-law of Dr. William Queen, in November or December last. Mr. Thompson resides with his father-in-law, and his place is about five miles southwesterly from Bryantown, near the lower edge of what is known as Zechiah Swamp. Mr. Thompson told me at the time that Booth was looking out for lands in this neighborhood or in this county, he said he was not very particular where, if he could get such a lot as he wanted, whether it was in Charles, Prince George, or Saint Marys county; and Booth inquired if I knew any parties in this neighborhood who had any fine horses for sale. I told him there was a neighbor of mine who had some very fine traveling horses, and he said he thought if he could purchase one reasonable he would do so, and would ride up to Washington on him instead of riding in the stage. The next evening he rode to my house and staid with me that night, and the next morning he purchased a rather old horse, but a very fine mover of Mr. George Gardiner, Sr., who resides but a short distance from my house. I would know the horse if I should see him again. He is a darkish bay horse, not bright bay, with a tolerably large head and had a defect in one eye. Booth gave eighty dollars for the horse. I have never seen Booth since that time to my knowledge until last Saturday night.

When I assisted the wounded man into my house on Saturday morning last, the other party with him who appeared to be very youthful, took charge of the horse and said he would keep it and the other one until they could be put in the stable. As soon as I could I woke my colored man Frank Washington, and sent him out to put the horses in the stable, and the young man came into the house. After setting the wounded man's leg the best I could for the time, I think I walked around to my farm-yard and gave some directions, when I returned breakfast was ready; and this young man was up and knocking about. I asked him to come to breakfast. He did so, but the other man remained up stairs in bed. I did not know who this young man was, but he remarked that he had seen me. He appeared to be a very fast young man and was very talkative. He was about five feet two or three inches high I would not be positive as to his height. He had a smooth face and appeared as if he had never shaved, his hair was black; and I should consider his complexion dark. I did not notice his eyes very particularly. He wore a dark-colored business coat. I have seen the photograph of Harold, but I do not recognize it as that of the young man. He seemed to be well acquainted throughout the whole country, and I asked his name; he gave it as Henson, and that of the wounded man as Tyser or Tyson. I did not hear either of them address the other by the first name.

The only thing that excited my suspicions on reflecting upon these circumstances was that after breakfast, when I was about to leave for my farm-work, this young man asked me if I had a razor about the house that his friend desired to take a shave, as perhaps he would feel better. I had noticed that the wounded man had whiskers and a moustache when he came into the house. After dinner, I went to see the patient and although he kept his face partly turned away from me I noticed that he had lost his moustache, but still retained his whiskers. I did not pay sufficient attention to his beard to determine whether it was false or natural.

This young man asked me if I could fix up clumsily some crutches for his friend to hobble along with, and I went down to the old Englishman I had had there who had a saw and augur and he and I made a rude pair of crutches out of a piece of plank and sent them to him. This young man mentioned the names of several parties in this neighborhood whom he knew; among others, several here in Bryantown. He mentioned being in the store of William Moore; he did not say when. I think he said he knew Bean, who kept store here; and he knew very well Len Roby, Rufus Roby, & Major James Thomas, Sr. He inquired the way from my house to Bryantown, although he represented in the morning that they had come from Bryantown. He said he knew Parson Wilmer, who lives at a place called Piney Church, he said also that they had met two persons, a lady and gentleman, walking somewhere near Bryantown that morning, and inquired of them the way to my house, and that they also met a negro, but did not state where & that they also inquired of him the way to my place.

I saw only one of the horses which these men rode to my house. She was a bay mare, moderately long tail, dark mane and tail. I won't be certain whether she had a star in the forehead or not, she appeared to be a meddlesome, high-spirited animal. I saw her after dinner, between twelve and one o'clock, when this young man and I rode over to my father's place in order to see if we could get a carriage for the wounded man; but I found that the carriages were all out of repair except one and we could not get that one. He then concluded to go to Bryantown for a conveyance to get his friend over as far as his friend's Mr. Wilmer's. I then went down to Mr. Hardy's, and was in conversation with him fully an hour when I returned home leisurely, and found the two men were just in the act of leaving. The young man inquired of me the nearest way to Mr. Wilmer's. I told them there were two ways; one was by the public road leading by Beantown; the other led across the swamp directly across from me by which they could save a mile both are easterly. This road from my house is directly across in a strait (sic) line; it is not a public way, but by taking down a fence you can get through. They concluded to take this latter route, and I gave them the necessary directions. I did not see them leave my house. The man on crutches had the house when I got back, and he was some fifty to seventy yards from me when this young man came to me and began to inquire of me the direction. I do not know how or where Booth got a conveyance away from my house; he did not go in a carriage, but he undoubtedly went on horseback.

When they came there in the morning this young man said that one of the horses would not stand without tying and asked that both of them should be put in the Stable. He held one of the horses until I returned into the house with the wounded man, when I called a colored boy named Frank Washington and sent him round to take the horses to the Stable. I have also a white man named Thomas Davis, who has charge of my horses, and I judge that he saw the horses which were in the Stable during Saturday.

I judge that between four and five o'clock on Saturday afternoon they left my house. I do not know where they went, I have not been spoken to by any one for professional advice in their behalf since that time, and have not seen either of them since.

It is about four miles across from my house to Parson Wilmer's, and by the public road it is about five miles. I suppose they could go in about an hour or an hour and a half by walking their horses.

I suppose in a day or two swelling would take place in the wounded man's leg; there was very little tumifaction in the wound, and I could discover crepitation very distinctly. It would be necessary to dress it again in two or three days if it were left in a recumbent posture, but if moved at a moderate rate, I do not know as it would aggravate it very much unless it was struck by something. I do not know much about wounds of that sort; a military surgeon would know more about those things.

Sam'l. A. Mudd

Subscribed and sworn before me this
22nd day of April 1865 H. H. Wells
Col. & P. M. Genl Def. S. of P

APPENDIX

ANDREW JOHNSON'S PARDON OF DR. MUDD

Andrew Johnson, President of the United States of America.
To all to Whom these Presents shall come, Greeting:

Whereas, on the twenty-ninth day of June in the year 1865, Dr. Samuel A. Mudd was by the judgment of a Military Commission, convened and holden at the City of Washington, in part convicted, and in part acquitted, of the specification wherein he was inculpated in the charge for the trial of which said Military Commission was so convened and held, and which specification in its principal allegation against him, was and is in the words and figures following, to wit: "And in further prosecution of said conspiracy, the said Samuel A. Mudd did, at Washington City and within the Military Department and military lines aforesaid, on or before the sixth day of March, A. D. 1865 and on divers other days and times between that day and the twentieth day of April A. D. 1865, advise, encourage, receive, entertain, harbor and conceal, aid and assist, the said John Wilkes Booth, David E. Herold, Lewis Payne, John H. Surratt, Michael O'Laughlen, George A. Atzerodt, Mary E. Surratt and Samuel Arnold and their confederates, with knowledge of the murderous and traitorous conspiracy aforesaid, and with intent to aid, abet, and assist them in the execution thereof, and in escaping from justice after the murder of the said Abraham Lincoln, in pursuance of said conspiracy in manner aforesaid:

And whereas, upon a consideration and examination of the record of said trial and conviction and of the evidence given at said trial, I am satisfied that the guilt found by the said judgment against the Samuel A. Mudd was of receiving, entertaining, harboring, and concealing John Wilkes Booth and David E. Herold, with the intent to aid, abet and assist them in escaping from justice after the assassination of the late President of the United States, and not of any other or greater participation or complicity in said abominable crime;

And whereas, it is represented to me by respectable and intelligent members of the medical profession, that the circumstances of the surgical aid to the escaping assassin and the imputed concealment of his flight are deserving of a lenient construction as within the obligations of professional duty, and thus inadequate evidence of a guilty sympathy with the crime or the criminal;

And whereas, in other respects the evidence, imputing such guilty sympathy or purpose of aid in defeat of justice, leaves room for uncertainty as to the true measure and nature of the complicity of the said Samuel A. Mudd, in the attempted escape of said assassins;

And whereas, the sentence imposed by said Military Commission upon the said Samuel A. Mudd was that he be imprisoned at hard labor for life, and the confinement under such sentence was directed to be had in the military prison at Dry Tortugas, Florida, and the said prisoner has been hitherto, and now is, suffering the infliction of such sentence;

And whereas, upon occasion of the prevalence of the Yellow Fever at that military station, and the death by that pestilence of the medical officer of the Post, the said Samuel A. Mudd devoted himself to the care and cure of the sick, and interposed his courage and his skill to protect the garrison, otherwise without adequate medical aid, from peril and alarm, and thus, as the officers and men unite in testifying, saved many valuable lives and earned the admiration and the gratitude of all who observed or experienced his generous and faithful service to humanity;

And whereas, the surviving families and friends of the Surgeon and other officers who were the victims of the pestilence earnestly present their dying testimony to the conspicuous merit of Dr. Mudd's conduct, and their own sense of obligation to him and Lieut. Zabriskie and two hundred and ninety nine noncommissioned officers and privates stationed at the Dry Tortugas have united in presenting to my attention the praiseworthy action of the prisoner and in petitioning for his pardon;

And whereas the Medical Society of Hartford County, Maryland, of which he was an associate, have petitioned for his pardon, and thirty nine members of the Senate and House of Representatives of the Congress of the United States have also requested his pardon; Now, therefore be it known that I, Andrew Johnson, President of the United States of America, in consideration of the premises, divers other good and sufficient reasons me there unto moving, do hereby grant to the said Dr. Samuel A. Mudd a full and unconditional pardon.

In testimony thereof, I have hereunto signed my name and caused the Seal of the United States to be affixed.

Done at the City of Washington, this Eight day of February, A. D. (Seal) 1869, and the Independence of the United States the ninety third.

ANDREW JOHNSON
By the President
WILLIAM H. SEWARD
Secretary of State

APPENDIX

4

PRESIDENT JIMMY CARTER'S LETTER TO DR. RICHARD D. MUDD, JANUARY 24, 1979.

THE WHITE HOUSE
WASHINGTON

July 24, 1979

To Dr. Richard Mudd

I am aware of your efforts to clear the name of your grandfather, Dr. Samuel Alexander Mudd, who set the broken leg of President Lincoln's assassin, John Wilkes Booth, and who was himself convicted as a conspirator in the assassination. Your persistence in these efforts, extending over more than a half century, is a tribute to your sense of familial love and dedication and is a credit to the great principles upon which our nation was founded.

Your petition and the petitions submitted to me on behalf of your grandfather by numerous members of Congress, several state legislatures, historians and private citizens have been exhaustively considered by my staff over the past two years. Regrettably, I am advised that the findings of guilt and the sentence of the military commission that tried Dr. Mudd in 1865 are binding and conclusive judgments, and that there is no authority under law by which I, as President, could set aside his conviction. All legal authority vested in the President to act in this case was exercised when President Andrew Johnson granted Dr. Mudd a full and unconditional pardon on February 8, 1869.

Nevertheless, I want to express my personal opinion that the declarations made by President Johnson in pardoning Dr. Mudd substantially discredit the validity of the military commission's judgment.

While a pardon is considered a statement of forgiveness and not innocence, the Johnson pardon goes beyond a mere absolution of the crimes for which Dr. Mudd was convicted. The pardon states that Dr. Mudd's guilt was limited to aiding the escape of President Lincoln's assassins and did not involve any other participation or complicity in the assassination plot itself—the crime for which Dr. Mudd was actually convicted. But President Johnson went on to express his doubt concerning even Dr. Mudd's criminal guilt of aiding Lincoln's assassins in their escape by stating:

"...it is represented to me by intelligent and respectable members of the medical profession that the circumstances of the surgical aid to the escaping of the assassin and the imputed concealment of his flight are deserving of a lenient construction, as within the obligations of professional duty and, thus, inadequate evidence of a guilty sympathy with the crime or the criminal;

"And...in other respects the evidence, imputing such guilty sympathy or purpose of aid in defeat of justice, leaves room for uncertainty as to the true measure and nature of the complicity of the said Samuel A. Mudd in the attempted escape of said assassins..."

A careful reading of the information provided to me about this case led to my personal agreement with the findings of President Johnson. I am hopeful that these conclusions will be given widespread circulation which will restore dignity to your grandfather's name and clear the Mudd family name of any negative connotation or implied lack of honor.

Sincerely,
signed Jimmy Carter

APPENDIX

5

PRESIDENT RONALD REAGAN'S LETTER TO DR. RICHARD D. MUDD (DECEMBER 8, 1987).

THE WHITE HOUSE
WASHINGTON

December 8, 1987

Dear Dr. Mudd:

I have investigated the situation with regard to your grandfather, Dr. Samuel Alexander Mudd. I know how much you have done and the effort you've put forth to get his name cleared of the charge against him. I regret to say I've learned that, as President, there is nothing I can do. Presidential power to pardon is all that is within a President's prerogatives and that, of course, was done by President Andrew Johnson.

Believe me, I'm truly sorry I can do nothing to help you in your long crusade. In my efforts to help, I came to believe as you do that Dr. Samuel Mudd was indeed innocent of any wrongdoing. But we'll have to accept that "full unconditional pardon" is what we must settle for.

Sincerely,
signed Ronald Reagan

APPENDIX

6

"LOST" STATEMENT OF GEORGE A. ATZERODT[1], STATEMENT OF GEO. A. ATZERODT TO PROV. MAR. MCPHAIL IN PRESENCE OF JOHN L. SMITH ON THE NIGHT OF MAY 1, 1865 BET. 8 & 10 PM.

James Wood[2] sometimes called Mosby boarded with Mrs. Murray an Irish woman on the corner of 9 & F St. in a three story house, front on the upper end of the P.O. and South End of Patent Office—with basement entrance on the left side going up 9th St. from Avenue. He was a little over six feet, black hair, smooth round face, gray coat black pants, & spring coat mixed with white & gray. Saw him last time on Friday evening about 5 o'ck with Booth. He sent for letters to the post office with James Hall. He was brought from New York. Surratt told me so. He said he had been a prisoner in Balte. near the depot. He was arrested for whipping a negro woman. Mosby was Wood's nick name—did not know him by any other name than mentioned. Gust. Powell now arrested in Old Capitol was one of the party. He went also by name of Gustavus Spencer, Surratt and Spencer came from Richmond, together just after it had fallen.

James Donaldson, a low chunky man about 23 or 24 years of age, small-potted, dark complexion (not very) deep plain black suit; only saw him one time & this was Wednesday previous to the murder, he was having an interview with Booth and told him to meet him on Friday eve & he replied he would and left and went up Penn. Avenue towards the Treasury building. I was under the impression he came on with Booth.

Arnold, O'Laughlin, Surratt, Harold, Booth and myself met once at a saloon or restaurant on the Aven. bet 13 & 14 St.

The Saml. Thomas registered on the morning of the 15th April at Penn Hotel, I met on my way to hotel, he was an entire Stranger to me. I left the Hotel alone on the morning of 15th of April. A Lieut. in room No. 51 will prove this. Surratt bought a boat from Dick Smoot & James Brawner living about Port Tobacco, for which they paid $300.00 and was to give one hundred Dolls. extra for taking care of it till wanted. Booth told me that Mrs. Surratt went to Surrattsville to get out the guns (Two Carbines) which had been taken to that place by Herold, This was Friday. The carriage was hired at Howards.

I saw a man named Weightman[3] who boarded at Surratt's at Post Office. he told me he had to go down the Country with Mrs. Surratt. This was on Friday, Also.

I am certain Dr. Mudd knew all about it, as Booth sent (as he told me) liquors & provisions for the trip with the President to Richmond, about two weeks before the murder to Dr. Mudd's.

Booth never said until the last night (Friday) that he intended to kill the President.

Herold came to the Kirkwood House, same evening for me to go to see Booth. I went with Herold & saw Booth. He then said he was going to kill the President and Wood, the Secy. of State. I did not believe him. This occurred in the evening about 7 1/2 o'clock. It was dark. I took a room at Kirkwood's. Both Herold & I went to the room left Herold's coat, knife, & pistol in room and never again returned to it. Booth said during the day that the thing had failed and proposed to go to Richmond & open the theatre. I am not certain but I think I stayed one night at Kirkwood's (Thursday) we were to try and get papers to Richmond from Mr. Johnson.

Booth spoke of getting the papers. He would get them out of the Theatre. Wood & Booth were apparently confidential with each other. Plenty of parties in Charles County knew of the kidnapping affair.

One of the men named Charles Yates, knew all about it, he went to Richmond during the winter he was to row the Presdt & party over.

Thos. Holborn[4] was to meet us on the road and help in the kidnapping. Bailey & Barnes knew nothing of the affair unless Booth told Bailey & he told Barnes. Booth had met Bailey on "C" St. with me. I did not meet Booth or any other of the party in Baltimore on or about the 31 of March.

Boyle[5] also killed Capt. Watkins near Annapolis last month, was one of the party, in the conspiracy.

I repeat I never knew anything about the murder.

I was intended to give assistance to the kidnapping. They come to Port Tobacco (Surratt & Booth) several times and brought me to Washington.- The pistol given me I sold or received a loan on it Saturday morng after the murder from John Caldwick[6] at Matthews & Wells, Store, High St. Georgetown. The knife I threw away just above Mrs. Canby's boarding house the night of the murder about 11 o'clock when I took my horse to stable. I had the horse out to help to take the President. I did not believe he was going to be killed, although Booth had said so. After I heard of the murder I run about the city like a crazy man.

I have not seen Arnold for some time, but saw O'Laughlin on Thursday evening, on the Avenue at Saloon near near U. S. Hotel. He told me he was going to see Booth.

Wood did not go on the street in day time for fear of arrest. When he first came to Washington he boarded at Surratt's. This was in Feby. He (Wood) went with Booth last of February to N. York.

Booth we understood paid the way. I know nothing about Canada. Wood told me he had horses in Virginia. Saml. Arnold & Mike O'Laughlin ought to know where the horses and pistols were bought.

Sam & Mike have a buggy and horse kept at stable in rear of Theatre. Booth had several horses at same place. I think the horses property was in Surratt's name. I sold one of the horses & paid part of the money to Booth and part to Herold, who said he would see Booth about it. The saddle and bridle belonging to Booth is at Penn House, where I left it. I overheard Booth when in conversation with Wood say, That he visited a chamber-maid at Seward's House & that she was pretty. He said he had a great mind to give her his diamond pin. Herold talked about powders & medicines on Friday night at Mrs. Condby's. Wood, Herold, Booth & myself were present. This was a meeting place because Wood could not go out for fear of arrest.

Kate Thompson or Kate Brown, as she was known by both names, put up at National & was well known at Penn House. She knew all about the affair. Surratt went to Richd with her last March & Gust. Howell made a trip with her to same place. This woman is about twenty yrs of age, good looking and well dressed. Black hair and eyes, round face from South Carolina & a widow.

I did not see Surratt for seven or eight days before the murder nor have I seen him since.

Miss Thompson or Brown had two large light trunks, one much larger than the other. Young Weightman at Surratts' ought to know about this woman. This remark made by me in Baltimore on the 31 of March alluded to blockade running & privateering altogether & Booth said he had money to buy a steamer & wanted me to go in it.

I was to be one of them. In this way I was going to make a pile of money.

Booth said he had met a party in N. York who would get the Prest. certain. They were going to mine the end of Kirk House, next to War Dept. They knew an entrance to accomplish it through. Spoke about getting friends of the Presdt. to get up an entertainment & they would mix in it, have a serenade &c & thus get at the Presdt. & party.

These were understood to be projects.

Booth said if he did not get him quick the N. York crowd would. Booth knew the New York party apparently by a sign. He saw Booth give some kind of sign to two parties on the Avenue who he said were from New

York. My Uncle Mr. Richter and family in Monty. Co. Md. knew nothing about the affair either before or after the occurrence & never suspected me of any thing wrong as I was in the habit of visiting and working in the neighborhood & staying with him. My father formerly owned part of the property now owned by Richter. Finis.

APPENDIX

7

AFFIDAVIT OF GEORGE W. DUTTON CONCERNING CERTAIN STATEMENTS MADE BY DR. SAMUEL A. MUDD, SINCE HIS TRIAL.

Camp Fry, Washington, D.C.
August 22, 1865.

Sir - I am in receipt of your communication of this date, in which you request information as regards the truthfulness of certain statements and confessions reported to have been made by Dr. Mudd while under my charge, en route to the Dry Tortugas.

In reply, I have the honor to state that my duties required me to be constantly with the prisoners, and during a conversation with Dr. Mudd, on the 22nd of July, he confessed that he knew Booth when he came to his house with Herold, on the morning after the assassination of the President; that he had known Booth for some time but was afraid to tell of his having been at his house on the 15th of April fearing that his own and the lives of his family would be endangered thereby. He also confessed that he was with Booth at the National Hotel on the evening referred to by Weichmann in his testimony; and that he came to Washington on that occasion to meet Booth by appointment, who wished to be introduced to John Surratt; that when he and Booth were going to Mrs. Surratt's house to see John Surratt, they met, on Seventh street, John Surratt, who was introduced to Booth, and they had a conversation of a private nature. I will here add that Dr. Mudd had with him a printed copy of the testimony pertaining to his trial, and I had, upon a number of occasions, referred to the same. I will also state that this confession was voluntary, and made without solicitation, threat or promise, and was made after the destination of the prisoners was communicated to them, which communication affected Dr. Mudd more than

the rest; and he frequently exclaimed, "Oh, there is now no hope for me."
"Oh, I can not live in such a place."

Please acknowledge receipt of this letter.

I am, General, very respectfully,
Your obedient servant,
George W. Dutton
Capt. Co. C, 10th Reg't. V. R. C., com'dg. Guard.

Sworn and acknowledged at Washington, D. C., this 23rd August, 1865, before me.

G. C. Thomas,
Notary Public.

APPENDIX

1. That I confessed to having known Booth while in my house; was afraid to give information of the fact, fearing to endanger my life, or made use of any language in that connection—I positively and emphatically declare to be notoriously false.

2. That I was satisfied and willingly acquiesced in the wisdom and decision of the Military Commission who tried me, is again notoriously erroneous and false. On the contrary I charged it (the Commission) with irregularity, injustice, usurpation, and illegality. I confess to being animated at the time, but have no recollection of having apologized.

3. I did confess to a casual or accidental meeting with Booth in front of one of the hotels on Pennsylvania Avenue, Washington, D. C., on December 23rd, 1864, and not on January 15th, 1865, as testified to by Weichmann. Booth, on that occasion, desired me to give him an introduction to Surratt, from whom he said he wished to obtain a knowledge of the country around Washington, in order to be able to select a good locality for a country residence. He had the number, street, and name of John Surratt written on a card, saying to comply with his request would not detain me over five minutes. (At this time I was not aware that Surratt was a resident to Washington). I declined at first, stating that I was with a relative and friend from the country and was expecting some friends over from Baltimore, who intended going down with me to spend Christmas, and was by appointment expected to be at the Pennsylvania House by a certain hour—eight o'clock. We started down one street, and then up another, and had not gone far when we met Surratt and Weichmann.

Introductions took place, and we turned back in the direction of the hotel. Arriving there, Booth insisted on our going to his room and taking something to drink with him, which I declined for reasons mentioned; but finding that Weichmann and Surratt were disposed to accept, I yielded, remarking that I could not remain many minutes. After arriving in the room, I took the first opportunity presented to apologize to Surratt for having introduced to him Booth—a man I knew so little concerning. This conversation took place in the passage in front of the room and was not over three minutes in duration. Whilst Surratt and myself were in the hall, Booth and Weichmann were sitting on the sofa in a corner of the room looking over some Congressional documents. Surratt and myself returned and resumed our former seats (after taking drinks ordered) around a centre table, which stood midway the room and distant seven or eight feet from Booth and Weichmann. Booth remarked that he had been down in the country a few days before, and said he had not yet recovered from the fatigue. Afterward he said he had been down in Charles County, and had made me an offer for the purchase of my land, which I confirmed by an affirmative answer; and he further remarked that on his way up he lost his way and rode several miles off the track. When he said this he left his seat and came over and took a seat immediately by Surratt; taking from his pocket an old letter, he began to draw lines, in order to ascertain from Surratt the location and description of the roads. I was a mere looker on.

Appendix

Report of Lieutenant Alexander Lovett.

Washington DC, April 29, 1865.
Major James R. O'Beirne
Provost marshal DC

Major

I have the honor to submit the following report of service in pursuit and detection of the assassin of the President, and persons implicated in the assassination.

In accordance with your order I started on the night of Monday the 17th inst. with officers Simon Gavacan and William Williams and 9 mounted men of Provisional Cavalry and proceeded to Surattsville (sic) Prince Georges Co. Md. for the purpose of arresting any parties implicated in the late assassination. At this place we were joined by Officers Lloyd and Cottingham, left the latter at Surattsville (sic) and proceeded toward Newport Tuesday morning the 18th. Having ascertained that John M. Lloyd a resident in the vicinity, was suspected of being in complicity with the assassination, I arranged his arrest which was accomplished on Tuesday P.M. on the road between Newport and T. B. about 2 miles beyond the latter place. After his arrest, he made a partial confession to me in private of his implication in the crime, stating that he knew the whole party and to save himself would "come out" on all of them, and that though he supposed he might be hung, he would not hesitate to tell all he knew of the affair. He said he was acquainted with Booth and Harrold (sic), who had frequently visited his home before the murder, and had had their arms concealed in his (house) for a week or ten days before it was committed.

On Friday morning the 14th inst. Mrs. Sarrat (sic) called at his house and told him that the party engaged in the plot would be along that night requesting him to furnish them with the arms (secreted) with him. Booth and Harrold (sic) came along and stopped at his house between 12 and 1 o'clock that night and took the arms secreted there with him, with the exception of one piece a seven shooter carbine which Booth could not carry on account of sickness resulting from a fractured leg. His confession was much confused as he was very agitated and frightened and cried most of the time. He was left in confinement at Roby's P. O. under charge of Officer Cottingham.

We then proceeded on Wednesday the 19th to Bryantown where we obtained information which led us to suppose that Booth had his leg dressed by Dr. Samuel Mudd who resided about 4 1/2 miles distant. We started for his residence where we arrested the said Dr. Mudd. He stated that two men came to his house about daybreak on Saturday morning, April 15th, one mounted on a bay horse, and the other on a roan. One of them was assisted into his house, and requested to have his leg set, which he said had been broken by his horse falling upon him. Booth seemed very much excited and declined any further explanation of the accident. After the operation of setting the leg, the patient asked for a razor and soap and water with which he shaved off his moustache. He then asked if he could obtain a buggy anywhere in the neighborhood. Dr. Mudd tried to get a buggy from his father, but did not suceed (sic). They remained until about 3 or 4 o'clock P. M. during which time he had a pair of crutches made for the injured man. When he was helped upon his horse and in company with his accomplice was piloted through the swamp by Dr. Mudd himself. The doctor said he left them after passing through the swamp and that was the last he saw of them. Before being asked if he knew Booth, he at first denied that he did, but afterwards acknowledged that he did, having been around the neighborhood with him last fall, and in introducing to different parties, that he was with him when he purchased a horse from Squire Gardiner and that he was satisfied the injured man was Booth when he set his leg. I obtained a boot which was cut from Booth's foot in order to set his leg. Inside was the name "J. Wilkes." I took the prisoner to Bryantown and turned him over to Col. Wells commanding at that place.

I am Major Very
Respectfully
your obt. Sevt.
Alexander Lovett (signed)
1st Lt. 14th Co. 2 Bat. VRC

Official Copy
Jas. R. O'Beirne
Maj. 22d Rgt VRC
and Pro Mar. DC

APPENDIX

10

OBITUARY OF SAMUEL A. MUDD.

Of interest in this brief biography of Mudd following his death is the statement that many residents of Charles County believed Mudd to have been a Confederate agent involved in the "forwarding of supplies and information."

Baltimore American, January 13, 1883

DR. MUDD DEAD
Wilkes Booth's Physician

The Man Who Set the Broken Leg of Lincoln's Assassin—His Trial and Sentence to the Dry Tortugas—How He Won a Pardon by His Heroism.

Dr. Samuel A. Mudd, who was sentenced to the Dry Tortugas for life for harboring J. Wilkes Booth, the assassin of President Lincoln, and who was subsequently pardoned by President Johnson, died on Wednesday last at his residence near Bryantown, Charles County, Md., after a brief illness. The career of Dr. Mudd was one of unusual interest and his name will go down in history as one of those connected with the terrible tragedy of April 14, 1865. The story of Dr. Mudd's connection with the case is as follows: On the night of April 14th, after Booth shot President Lincoln, he fled in company with Harold. As is well known, the assassin in jumping from the private box in Ford's Theatre occupied by the President, to the stage, broke his ankle. Harold stood by his side and the two fled into Charles County, Maryland. When the pursuers of the assassin, following on his trail, reached the residence of Dr. Mudd near Bryantown, two days after the shooting, the Doctor admitted to them that about daybreak on the 15th two men rode rapidly up to his house, and one alighted. The stranger asked the Doctor to set the broken ankle of his companion, and the latter was then assisted from the horse into the Doctor's house where his injury was attended to. They remained at the house during the day and departed at night fall, and Dr. Mudd always contended that this was the beginning and ending of his acquaintance with them; that he did not know who they were, and did not hear of the shooting of the President until the next Sunday. One of the witnesses at the trial of the conspirators, however, testified that when he went to Dr. Mudd's house to arrest him, on April 21st, the physician, finding that they were going to search the house, told his wife to bring down stairs an old boot leg, which had been cut open in order to get it off the injured leg of Booth. Inside of the leg was written in ink, "J. Wilkes." Later in the day Dr. Mudd admitted that the injured man was Booth, and principally on this admission he was convicted. President Johnson sentenced him, together with Spangler, Arnold, and McLaughlin, to imprisonment in the Albany penitentiary for life at hard labor, and subsequently sent them to the Dry Tortugas. While at the Dry Tortugas Dr. Mudd made several attempts to escape, and on one occasion succeeded in concealing himself in the coal hold of a British steamship outward bound. Just before the steamship sailed, however, he was discovered and sent on shore. When he had passed two years of his life therewith yellow fever became epidemic, and the island was deserted of many of the residents and physicians. Dr. Mudd then came forward, and making known his profession, volunteered to attend the sick. For several months he worked hard, and at one time was the only physician on the island who dared attend the victims of the yellow scourge. When the disease died out the residents forwarded a petition for Dr. Mudd's pardon to President Johnson. This President Johnson granted, and Dr. Mudd returned home much broken in health, and resumed the practice of his profession in Charles county, where he resided until the day of his death. During the war he had always been an unqualified sympathizer with the Confederacy, and was believed by many to have been an agent of the Confederate government in this state, for the forwarding of supplies and information. His reputation as an unqualified secessionist, and the fact that on one occasion prior to the shooting of Lincoln he attended church at Port Tobacco in company with Booth, were the principal grounds upon which public opinion was influenced against him before and after his trial. "Dr. Mudd," it was stated by a Charles County gentleman in this city last night, "certainly never contemplated the assassination of Lincoln by Booth or any of his confederates, but he did expect the abduction of Lincoln, and was heart and soul in favor of it. When Booth's vanity led him to commit the deed he of course had no intention of stopping at Mudd's house. He was bound for the south, hoping to get through to South America and thence to Spain. When the assassin's leg was broken, however, he went to Dr. Mudd, knowing he would receive help and sympathy. This was, I think, the real state of Dr. Mudd's connection with the affair." From the time the doctor was sent to the Tortugas, his wife, who with her children, continued to reside in Bryantown, with untiring perseverance never relaxed her efforts to secure the pardon of her husband. She succeeded in interesting prominent public men throughout the country in the case, and would probably have secured Dr. Mudd's release eventually if the petition from Dry Tortugas had not hastened matters. Several years ago, when the yellow fever threatened to become epidemic in the South, Dr. Mudd went to Washington, and tendered his services to the National Board of Health as a consulting physician to treat the cases, believing that his experience with the disease in the Dry Tortugas would be of much value. The Board of Health, however, declined his offer. A claim for compensation for attending the federal soldiers ill with the fever on the Dry Tortugas was filed before Congress a few years ago by Dr. Mudd, but was disallowed. Dr. Mudd was born near Bryantown, and was about 48 years of age. He leaves a wife, the sister of the late Jere Dyer, of this city, and several children. Dr. Mudd's sister was married to Mr. Dyer, his wife's brother, and now resides in this city. He leaves two brothers, now living in Charles County—Messers. J. A. Mudd and H. L. Mudd, Jr., both prominent farmers. His father, Mr. H. L. Mudd, who died about ten years ago, was formerly quite wealthy, but the enormous expenses attending the defense of his son, when he was tried, it is said swept away nearly all the property. The father of the doctor was untiring in his efforts to save his son, and engaged the best counsel to be had, among the number being the present Judge Stone, who had charge of the defense. Dr. Mudd was a cousin of Dr. George Mudd, late Republican senator and quite a prominent public man. The deceased ran for the House of Delegates with Mr. Samuel Cox on the Democratic ticket in 1877.

Photographs by Edward Steers, Jr.

The tombstone of Dr. Samuel Alexander Mudd and his wife, Sarah Frances (Dyer) Mudd in the burial ground adjacent to St. Mary's Church. In this cemetery are the graves of Dr. Mudd's father and mother, Dr. Mudd's neighbor, George Gardiner, and Dr. William Queen, a member of the Confederate underground.

APPENDIX

11

THE SAMUEL A. MUDD RELIEF ACT OF 1997 AND H. R. 1885

105th CONGRESS
1st Session
H. R. 1885

To direct the Secretary of the Army to set aside the conviction of Dr. Samuel A. Mudd by a military commission in 1865 for aiding, abetting, and assisting the conspirators who assassinated President Abraham Lincoln.

IN THE HOUSE OF REPRESENTATIVES, June 12, 1997, Mr. Hoyer (for himself and Mr. Ewing) introduced the following bill; which was referred to the Committee on National Security - Subcommittee on Military Personnel

SECTION 1. FINDINGS.

The Congress finds the following:

(1) On June 29, 1865, Dr. Samuel A. Mudd of the State of Maryland was convicted by a military commission in Washington, D.C., of aiding, abetting, and assisting the conspirators who assassinated President Abraham Lincoln.

(2) The conviction of Dr. Mudd was based on evidence of guilt that fell so far short of meeting the prosecution's burden of proof that such conviction amounted to a denial of due process of law which was so extreme as to constitute fundamental unfairness.

(3) Because the conviction of Dr. Mudd was not based on sufficient evidence and resulted in a denial of due process of law, the Secretary of the Army should set aside the conviction.

SEC. 2. DIRECTION TO SET ASIDE CONVICTION.

The Secretary of the Army shall set aside the conviction of Dr. Samuel A. Mudd of the State of Maryland that was entered on June 29, 1865, for aiding, abetting, and assisting the conspirators who assassinated President Abraham Lincoln.

INTRODUCTION OF THE SAMUEL MUDD RELIEF ACT OF 1997

HON. STENY H. HOYER

in the House of Representatives THURSDAY, JUNE 12, 1997

Mr. HOYER: Mr. Speaker, I rise today to introduce legislation which seeks to clear the name of Dr. Samuel A. Mudd and set aside his conviction for harboring John Wilkes Booth, the assassin of President Abraham Lincoln. Due to the tremendous amount of controversy over Dr. Mudd's conviction, his case was reviewed by five high-ranking civilian employees of the Department of the Army in January, 1992. After all the testimony and evidence waspresented, the civilian panel unanimously declared Dr. Mudd innocent of the charges. However, without commenting on the facts in this case, the Acting Assistant Secretary of the Army declined to accept this decision based on jurisdictional grounds. I believe that Dr. Mudd deserves an official exoneration, and that the Department of the Army should follow the recommendations of its own civilian panel, and that of two former Presidents.

On April 14, 1865 President Lincoln was assassinated at Ford's Theater by the actor, John Wilkes Booth. Following the extensive manhunt for Booth that ensued, on April 21, 1865, Dr. Samuel Mudd, a gentleman farmer and physician, living in Southern Maryland, was arrested for 'aiding and comforting' Booth. Specifically, he was accused of setting Booth's leg which was broken when he jumped off the balcony onto the stage at Ford's Theater.

Dr. Mudd was represented by General Thomas Ewing, Jr., who served in the U.S. House of Representatives in the 1870's, representing Lancaster, OH. Because President Lincoln was also Commander in Chief, Dr. Mudd was tried before a military commission, known as the Hunter Commission. Although he was found guilty, Dr. Mudd was imprisoned, not hung as were four of Booth's alleged co-conspirators. After being imprisoned in the Dry Tortugas for 4 years, President Andrew Jackson pardoned him because of his devoted medical care of prisoners and guards in a yellow fever epidemic.

For more than 75 years now, Dr. Richard Mudd, the grandson of Dr. Samuel Mudd, has been working to have his grandfather's conviction set aside. He is now 96 years old and has devoted his entire adult life to this very important and worthy cause. His efforts to have the Department of the Army set aside the conviction have been, and continue to be, grounded in fact and have substantial support among historians throughout the Nation. Moreover, former Presidents Carter and Reagan have both written letters proclaiming their belief that Dr. Mudd was innocent.

In July, 1990, at the urging of Senator Biden, the Judge Advocate General of the U.S. Army determined that the U.S. Army Board of Correction of Military Records [ABCMR] had the jurisdiction to review such a case and to determine the feasibility of setting aside the conviction. For 2 years, the Mudd family collected historical information and prepared their case, which was presented to the Army in January, 1992. Their argument that Dr. Mudd's conviction should be set aside was based on the premise that the Army did not have jurisdiction over a civilian, who had a constitutional right to be tried by a jury of his peers in civil court. Moreover, his due process rights, they argued, had been violated because insufficient evidence of his guilt had been presented to the military commission.

Mr. Speaker, the five member board unanimously found that Dr. Mudd's conviction should be set aside and recommended such action to the Secretary of the Army. They had determined that the Hunter Commission of 1865 did not have the jurisdictional authority to try Dr. Samuel Mudd and that he had suffered a 'gross infringement of his constitutional rights.' These jurisdictional arguments were bolstered by a Supreme Court decision in 1886 (sic) that a citizen of the United States, who was not a member of the armed forces, could not be tried by the military when the civil courts are open and functioning. However, in a surprise decision in July, 1992, Acting Assistant Secretary William D. Clark declined to adopt the Board's recommendation. While this decision was appealed in August, 1992, no further action was taken until March, 1996.

In March, 1996, as over 130 years had passed since the assassination of President Lincoln, Assistant Secretary Sara Lister declined to adopt the board's recommendation to set aside Dr. Mudd's conviction, adding that her decision did not 'involve the substantive aspects of whether Dr. Mudd was actually guilty or innocent.' Rather, Assistant Secretary Lister found that it was improper to attempt to retry this case or determine the feasibility and appropriateness of a decision made over 100 years earlier. She thus found that she did not have the appropriate jurisdiction to set aside Dr. Mudd's conviction. She determined that 'It would be inappropriate for the Army to administratively correct the record of conviction or attempt to alter legal history by non-judicial means.'

However, Mr. Speaker, for those of us who believe that there is significant evidence and information proving Dr. Mudd's innocence, therefore agreeing with the ABCMR's 1992 decision, we cannot stand idly by and allow this conviction to stand. If the facts are clear and conclusive, as the ABCMR found in 1992 and as former Presidents Carter and Reagan have determined, then the Congress must act to set aside the conviction of an innocent man.

Despite the Army's claim that the appropriate time to appeal this decision was 130 years ago, we must understand the hysteria and upheaval that ensued immediately following President Lincoln's tragic assassination. It is clear that the pressure to round up and arrest all of those involved in the assassination led to a conviction that fell far short of meeting the prosecution's burden of proof requirement. Moreover, the process by which Dr. Mudd was found guilty clearly violated his constitutional right to a 'trial by jury.'

Governor Engler and state legislators from Michigan, including Senator William Van Regenmorter, and the Charles County Board of Commissioners in Maryland support efforts to have this conviction overturned. Moreover, there are hundreds of people throughout the Nation who are dedicated to seeing justice served and history recorded accurately in this case. I am introducing this legislation today with my colleague from Illinois, Representative Thomas Ewing, who himself is collaterally related to Samuel Mudd's lawyer. It directs the Secretary of the Army to set aside the conviction and specifically cites the denial of due process of law and insufficient evidence. Because Dr. Mudd was found guilty by a military court, his record can only be cleared by the U.S. Army.

Mr. Speaker, while it is clear that Dr. Mudd did set John Wilkes Booth's broken leg, there is absolutely no evidence to suggest that he was either a co-conspirator in the assassination of President Lincoln or even aware of the events which had occurred earlier that evening on Friday, April 14, 1865.

I urge my colleagues to join me in ensuring that history is recorded accurately and that our Nation's most basic individual rights, embodied in the Constitution, are not violated at any time. Dr. Samuel Mudd's name and honor and that of his family, many of whom live in my district, hangs in the balance. We ought to allow the findings and decision of the Army Board of Correction of Military Records, the most reputable and qualified entity to date which has reviewed this case, to stand, thus ending the 132-year-long disservice accorded to Dr. Samuel Mudd.

Selected Bibliography

Since the endnotes which appear throughout this book cite all of the bibliographical sources used in this study, a source bibliography is unnecessary. Instead, a selective bibliographical listing of those books which will give the reader a full exposure to the events and persons associated with the murder of President Abraham Lincoln is presented. Also recommended is the *Surratt Courier*, a newsletter published by the Surratt Society (P.O. Box 427) in Clinton, Maryland (20735). This longstanding publication has proven to be an indispensible source of materials relating to the assassination of Abraham Lincoln not available elsewhere.

Arnold, Samuel B. *Defense and Prison Experiences of a Lincoln Conspirator.* Hattiesburg, MS: Book Farm Press, 1943.

Basler, Roy P., ed. *The Collected Works of Abraham Lincoln.* 9 vols. New Brunswick, NJ: Rutgers University Press, 1953.

Bryan, George S. *The Great American Myth.* Reprint. Chicago: Americana House, Inc., 1990.

Hanchett, William. *The Lincoln Murder Conspiracies.* Urbana, IL: University of Illinois Press, 1983.

Higdon, Hal. *The Union vs. Dr. Mudd.* Chicago: Follett, 1964.

Jones, John Paul, ed., *Dr. Mudd and the Lincoln Assassination. The Case Reopened.* Conshohocken, PA: Combined Books, 1995.

Kauffman, Michael W., ed., *Samuel Bland Arnold: Memoirs of a Lincoln Conspirater.* Bowie, MD: Heritage Press, 1997.

Jones, Thomas A. *J. Wilkes Booth.* Chicago: Laird and Lee, 1893.

Kunhardt, Dorothy Meserve, and Philip B. Kunhardt, Jr. *Twenty Days.* New York: Harper and Row, 1965.

Lattimer, John K. *Kennedy and Lincoln: Medical and Ballistic Comparisons of Their Assassinations.* New York: Harcourt Brace Jovanovich, 1980.

McHale, John E. Jr. *Dr. Samuel A. Mudd and the Lincoln Assassination.* Parsippany, NJ: Dillon Press, 1995.

Mudd, Nettie. *The Life of Dr. Samuel A. Mudd.* New York: Neale Publishing Company, 1906.

Oldroyd, Osborn H. *The Assassination of Abraham Lincoln.* Washington: 1901.

Pitman, Benn. *The Assassination of President Lincoln and the Trial of the Conspirators.* Philip Van Doren Stern: 1865. Reprint. New York: Funk and Wagnalls, 1954.

Poore, Ben Perley, ed. *The Conspiracy Trial for the Murder of the President, and the Attempt to Overthrow the Government by the Assassination of its Principal Officers.* 3 vols. New York: Arno Press, 1972.

Roscoe, Theodore. *The Web of Conspiracy.* Englewood Cliffs, NJ: Prentice-Hall, 1959.

Steers, Edward Jr. *The Escape and Capture of John Wilkes Booth.* Gettysburg, PA: Thomas Publications, 1983.

Tidwell, William A., James O. Hall and David Winfred Gaddy. *Come Retribution.* Jackson, MS: University Press of Mississippi, 1988.

Verge, Laurie, ed. *From War Department Files. Statements Made by the Alleged Lincoln Conspirators Under Examination 1865.* Clinton, MD: Surratt Society, 1980.

Weckesser, Elden C. *His Name Was Mudd.* Jefferson: McFarland and Company, 1991.

Weichmann, Louis J. *A True History of the Assassination of Abraham Lincoln and of the Conspiracy of 1865.* ed. Floyd E. Risvold, New York: Alfred A. Knopf, 1975.

The primary sources used in this study are:

The Trial Transcript, microfilm 599, sixteen reels, National Archives; The AGO Reward File, microfilm 619, four reels, National Archives; and the extensive files of James O. Hall.

Notes

Introduction

1 Dr. Richard Dyer Mudd of Saginaw, Michigan, has devoted over seventy years to reversing the action of the military commission that tried his grandfather and found him guilty as an accomplice to John Wilkes Booth's assassination of Abraham Lincoln.

2 President Andrew Johnson issued Samuel A. Mudd a full pardon on February 8, 1869.

3 See Appendix 4.

4 See Appendix 3.

5 Clark Hughes, *Saginaw News*, December 15, 1987. Roger Mudd, while not a direct descendant of Samuel Mudd, is a collateral descendant.

6 See Appendix 5.

7 House Concurrent Resolution No. 126, Michigan legislature, *A Concurrent Resolution Expressing the Sentiment of the Michigan Legislature That Dr. Samuel A. Mudd Was Innocent of Any Complicity in the Assassination of President Abraham Lincoln*, July 17, 1973.

8 President Reagan was petitioned by other Mudd family members and not by Dr. Richard Mudd.

9 Letter from President Jimmy Carter to Dr. Richard D. Mudd, July 24, 1979, in the possession of Dr. Richard D. Mudd.

10 A presidential pardon goes beyond freeing a convicted individual or granting immunity from prosecution to one charged with a crime. It also relieves the individual of the consequences of his or her conviction. Thus, unlike a convicted felon, an individual so pardoned may vote, run for office, serve in the armed forces of the United States and enjoy all of the rights and privileges of an individual never charged or convicted of a crime. It does not, however, reverse the findings or conclusions of the individual's conviction as a result of his or her trial. In *ex parte Garland* (4 Wallace, December, 1866, 333) the Supreme Court stated that,"...in the eye of the law the offender is as innocent **as if** (emphasis added) he had never committed the offense." The court does not state that a presidential pardon views the offender as not having committed the offense. For a discussion of the meaning of a presidential pardon see Hall, James O., *Surratt Courier*, XX: No. 9, September, 1995.

11 Certain important primary documents reside in private collections, but photocopies have made their way into the public domain and public historical societies. The principal depository is the Surratt House Museum Library located in Clinton, Maryland.

Chapter 1

1 Fletcher's horse was named Charley. For Fletcher's account of the events on the night of April 14 see: Statement of John Fletcher, National Archives and Records Administration (hereafter abbreviated NARA), M599, reel 5, frames 414-421, and NARA, M619, reel 456, frames 299-307; also, Testimony of John Fletcher in Poore, Ben Perley, *The Conspiracy Trial for the Murder of the President*, I:326-341, New York: Arno Press, 1972, hereafter referred to as *Trial*.

2 Ibid., 328.

3 Now called the Anacostia River.

4   Testimony of Silas T. Cobb in *Trial*, I:252, and NARA, M-599, reel 4, frames 0172-0178.

5   The 22nd Army Corps occupied a series of sixty-nine forts and batteries which ringed the District of Columbia. It was responsible for protecting the city from Confederate attack. When Grant began his siege of Lee's army in front of Petersburg and Richmond, he stripped as many troops as he could from the Washington defenses where he felt they served little useful purpose. Most of the forts were now manned by skeleton crews of soldiers and invalid veterans known as the Veteran Reserve Corps.

6   Atzerodt, in fact, had not fled the city, but after wandering about, which including a trolley ride to the Navy Yard, he checked into his favorite hotel, the Pennsylvania House (also known as the Kimmel House). Rising early on Saturday morning, Atzerodt slowly made his way into Montgomery County, Maryland where he arrived at the home of his cousin Hartman Richter. Atzerodt was eventually taken into custody on Thursday, April 20. Statement of George A. Atzerodt, NARA, M-599, reel 2, frames 0045-0047.

7   The spot where Booth and Herold rendezvoused is believed to be at a point just over the District line known as Soper's Hill. It was located along the road to Surrattsville, now Clinton, Maryland. Statement of David E. Herold, NARA, M-599, reel 4, frames 0442-0485.

8   The one-eyed horse would be indirectly linked to Dr. Samuel A. Mudd who introduced Booth to its former owner, George Gardiner, Mudd's nearest neighbor. Booth purchased the horse from Gardiner in December 1864 during the second of his two known visits with Dr. Mudd in Charles County, Maryland. Statement of Samuel A. Mudd, NARA, M-599, reel 5, frames 0212-0225.

9   Letter from Michael Henry to James O'Beirne, provost marshall of the District of Columbia, July 20, 1865, in the collection of Scott A. Balthaser. Photocopy in author's files.

10 NARA, M-599, reel 15, frame 0067.

11 Testimony of David D. Dana, *Trial*, II:68. The Bryantown Tavern was known locally as the Montgomery Tavern after its proprietor.

CHAPTER 2

1   Lincoln had been a target of kidnappers and assassins from the first day of his election in the fall of 1860. As Lincoln traveled from Springfield to his inaugural in Washington in February 1861, the famous detective Alan Pinkerton had successfully aborted a plot to murder Lincoln as he passed through the city of Baltimore. Lincoln received dozens of letters threatening his life while in the White House. He kept several of these letters carefully tied with a ribbon in one of the small cubby holes in his desk, presumably for later reading.

2   Richard Taylor (1826 - 1879) distinguished himself by repulsing Major General Nathaniel P. Banks' Red River Expedition in 1864 by defeating Banks' Army of the Gulf at Mansfield and Pleasant Hill which effectively ended Banks' career in Louisiana. Taylor surrendered the last Confederate force east of the Mississippi River in May 1865.

3   The senior officer in command at Fort Donelson was the former secretary of war under President James Buchanan, John B. Floyd. Floyd's second-in-command was Confederate Brigadier General Gideon J. Pillow. Floyd decided to escape Donelson along with Pillow and turned command of the fort over to Brigadier General Simon Bolivar Buckner for purposes of the surrender. Floyd and Pillow slipped out of the fort at night and escaped under the protection of the famed Confederate cavalryman, Nathan Bedford Forrest.

4   Louthan, Henry T., "A Proposed Abduction of Lincoln," *Confederate Veteran*, June 1908, 157-158.

5   Ibid.,158.

6   The Soldiers' Home was located approximately three miles due north of the Capitol building situated in the rolling countryside outside the city proper. Lincoln, as James Buchanan before him, moved his family to a cottage at Soldiers' Home each year to avoid the hot, humid and disease-laden city during the summer months. The Lincolns spent nearly a fourth of their tenure in Washington living at the Home.

7   Taylor apparently crossed the Potomac River from the Virginia side using one of the two main routes the Confederates secured to move between Richmond and Washington. It was the very same route which Booth had planned to use in his abduction escape and did use in his own escape effort.

8   Louthan, 157.

9   Ibid., 158.

10 Ibid., 158.

11 Tidwell, William A., James O. Hall and David Winfred Gaddy, *Come Retribution: The Confederate Secret Service and the Assassination of Lincoln*, Jackson and London: University Press of Mississippi, 1988.

12 Lincoln himself doubted his reelection chances and documented his reservations by writing a note to the effect that it was not likely that his administration would be reelected. Lincoln asked each of his cabinet members to sign the note *in camera* and carefully put it away to be read at a later date should his feelings come true. Of course, he was wrong as were the naysayers who sought his replacement as the Republican candidate in 1864.

13 Hampton succeeded Major General J.E.B. Stuart to command of the Cavalry Corps of the Army of Northern Virginia following Stuart's death at Yellow Tavern on May 12, 1864. Hampton was only one of three civilians without formal military training (Richard Taylor being the second) to attain the rank of lieutenant general in the Confederate army.

14 Brennan, John C., "General Bradley T. Johnson's Plan to Abduct President Lincoln," *Chronicles of St. Mary's*, 22:413-424, 1974. Also Johnson, Bradley T., "My Ride Around Baltimore in Eighteen Hundred and Sixty-Four," *Cavalry Journal*, September 1889, 250-260.

15 White's Ford was located substantially west of the District near Poolesville in Montgomery County, Maryland, and served as a major crossing point for Confederates from Virginia into Maryland. Mosby and certain of his command had crossed into Montgomery County here on several occasions.

16 Soldiers' Home consisted of a large main hall which housed the old inmates and three residences or cottages which normally housed the Home's administrators. The Lincolns stayed in the largest cottage named for Major Robert Anderson of Sumter fame who had been the Home's first administrator. The Stanton family occasionally stayed in a smaller cottage previously used by James Buchanan as his summer retreat.

17 Gautier's Restaurant was located on Pennsylvania Avenue near Twelfth Street, a half block from the Kirkwood Hotel and three blocks from Ford's Theatre.

18 Arnold, Samuel B., *Defense of a Lincoln Conspirator*, Hattiesburg, Mississippi: Book Farm, 1943.

19 Lincoln canceled his trip to Campbell Hospital at the urging of Indiana Governor Oliver P. Morton so that Lincoln could accompany Morton to the National Hotel where Morton and Lincoln received the captured flag from the 142nd Indiana Volunteer Infantry Regiment.

20 Washington *Evening Star*, March 18, 1865.

21 Atzerodt, *Lost Confession*. On May 1, 1865, while in custody at the Washington Arsenal, George Atzerodt gave a seven page statement to Baltimore Provost Marshal James McPhail. This statement, known today as the "Lost Confession," subsequently disappeared only to resurface in 1977. Joan L. Chaconas, past president of the Surratt Society, discovered the statement among the private papers of Captain William E. Doster, the court-appointed defense attorney for Atzerodt. A photocopy of the statement was secured. Subsequently the statement was sold at auction and resides in a private collection. Hereafter referred to as Atzerodt, *Lost Confession*. See Tidwell, William A., James O. Hall and David Winfred Gaddy, *Come Retribution*, Jackson: University Press of Mississippi, 1988, 416-418, for a full description of circumstances surrounding Atzerodt's lost confession. See Appendix 6 for full text.

22 Seward was recovering from a serious accident in which he had been thrown from his carriage and injured his neck nine days prior to the attempt on his life.

23 Testimony of Robert R. Jones, *Trial*, I: 110.

24 John T. Ford, owner of the theater, was away on business and not present when Booth visited the theater.

25 While visiting the theater that morning, Booth prepared for his murder attempt by hiding a piece of wood from a music stand and cutting a small hole in the plaster wall inside the outer box door. He would wedge the length of wood between the door and the wall securing it in the notch so that the door could not be forced open from the outside. Booth in effect, was locking himself inside the box with Lincoln and his guests.

26 This assumes that the power structure in Washington would be willing to deal for Lincoln. There are some who believe that getting Lincoln out of the way would result in an even harsher posture with the Confederate government and would result in federal authorities dragging their collective feet.

27 This became the justification for trying the accused conspirators before a military tribunal. See Speed, James, *Opinion of the Constitutional Power of the Military to Try and Execute the Assassins of the President*. Government Printing Office, Washington, 1865.

28 Louthan, Henry T., *Confederate Veteran*, 157 - 158.

29 Samuel Arnold, Michael O'Laughlen and Henry Atzerodt (brother to George Atzerodt, see NARA, M-599, reel 7, frame 0006, folder 2, containing a letter from Henry Atzerodt to George Atzerodt which is addressed to Dear Brother) were all members of Johnson's First Maryland Infantry and would have undoubtedly been among the chosen one hundred. See Brennan.

30 Gaddy, David W. "The Surratt Tavern — A Confederate "Safe House?"." *In Pursuit of...Continuing Research in the Field of the Lincoln Assassination*, Surratt Society, 1990, 129. This important document was discovered by Erick F. Davis among various Confederate papers in the National Archives.

31 Mudd's importance was to this second group, facilitating the escape to Virginia and hopefully, Richmond.

CHAPTER 3

1 "Thus Always to Tyrants," the motto of the state of Virginia. Booth is reported to have shouted this from the box immediately after firing the fatal shot. Others testified that he shouted from the stage after leaping from the box.

2 Statement of George A. Atzerodt, NARA, M-599, reel 3, frames 0596-0602.

3 Atzerodt, *Lost Confession*.

4 General Grant had originally accepted the president's invitation but then backed out after discussing it with Mrs. Grant. Julia Grant had suffered the insults of Mary Lincoln a month earlier during a visit to City Point at a military review and did not wish to experience such wrath again. The Grants left in the afternoon for New Jersey where their children were in school, and sent their regrets to the Lincolns. Booth knew this, having seen the Grants leave earlier in the day according to the statement of John Matthews. Grant, along with Major General Ambrose Burnside, had accompanied Lincoln to a performance at Ford's Theatre a month earlier where they saw Booth's brother-in-law, John Sleeper Clarke, star in a farce entitled, "Love In Livery." See *Evening Star*, "The President and General Grant at Ford's," February 11, 1865, 2, col. 6.

5 Statement of David Herold, NARA, M-599, reel 4, frames 0442-85. This statement is reproduced in *From War Department Files*, Laurie Verge, ed., Surratt Society, Clinton, Maryland, 1980, 1-21.

6 Powell would run from the house after thinking he had murdered most of the residents including Seward, and mounting his horse, ride toward the Navy Yard Bridge. He apparently became lost and abandoned his horse in the eastern part of the city and is believed to have hidden out in Glenwood Cemetery or Congressional Cemetery not far from the bridge. When arrested on Monday, April 17, at Mary Surratt's boarding house, Powell was carrying a pickax suggesting he had been hiding out in one of the two nearby cemeteries where such implements may have been available.

7 Edman Spangler was accused of being an accomplice in Booth's crime and received a sentence of six years' imprisonment. Witnesses testified that Spangler quickly shut the rear door of Ford's after Booth dashed through it, thus aiding Booth's escape. Spangler served three and a half years of his sentence together with Dr. Mudd, Samuel Arnold and Michael O'Laughlen at Fort Jefferson before being pardoned in 1869 by Andrew Johnson. Spangler returned to the farm of Dr. Mudd where he lived for the next six years before dying in 1875. He lies buried in the old cemetery of St. Peters Church, the church attended by Dr. Mudd.

8 Joseph "Peanuts" Burroughs was a young boy who served as a "gopher" running various errands for the staff and selling peanuts on the sidewalk in front of the theater, hence the name, "Peanuts" Burroughs. For his actions on the night of April 14, 1865, see *Trial*, I, 225-233.

9 Earlier in the day, Ford had the temporary partition separating the two boxes removed creating a single large box instead of two smaller boxes.

10 Lincoln was accompanied to the theater that night by John F. Parker, a member of the D.C. police force who served as one of his personal bodyguards. Parker was absent at the time Booth approached the box, but Lincoln's personal valet, Charles Forbes was sitting in the seat closest to the door. Parker was later charged by a police board of inquiry for failure to protect the president, but was acquitted of all charges and reinstated on the police force. Ironically, Forbes was a signatory to the charges leveled against Parker for "neglect of duty." Photocopy in author's files, original in a private collection.

11 Testimony of Theodore McGowan, *Trial*, I:194. For further details, see statement of Captain T. McGowen, NARA, M-599, reel 5, frame 0317 - 0322; and statement of Lieutenant A. M. Crawford, NARA, M-599, reel 7, frame 0481 - 0483. Both were seated near the door to the presidential box and saw Booth enter.

12 Translates to "Thus always to tyrants," the motto of the state of Virginia. Historical legend has Booth shouting this famous motto from the stage after his

jump from the box, but testimony given within a few hours of the event have him shouting the motto from the box after firing the fatal shot. Others claim he shouted something to the effect that, " The South is avenged!" from the stage after he gathered himself up following his dramatic jump. For a detailed discusson of eyewitness accounts of Booth's words see, Good, Timothy S., ed., *We Saw Lincoln Shot. One Hundred Eyewitness Accounts,* Jackson: University Press of Mississippi, 1995.

13 A national standard was originally on display as the flag which "avenged the martyred President" by ensnaring Booth thus causing him to land off balance and break his leg. That flag has disappeared, but a photograph of it while on display still exists in the National Park Service collection (Oldroyd Collection) which adds further to the mystery of which flag caught Booth and led him to seek medical assistance from Dr. Mudd.

14 For an alternate account of how Booth broke his leg see, Kauffman, Michael W., "Booth's Escape Route: Lincoln's Assassin On The Run," *Blue & Gray Magazine,* June, 1990, 17.

15 See testimony of Silas T. Cobb in *Trial,* Vol. I, 1865, 251.

16 Beantown is within the same neighborhood where Dr. Mudd's farm was located. Mudd stated that he lived "...near Bryantown," which was situated approximately five miles due south of Mudd's house. Beantown was situated approximately four miles due west of Mudd's.

17 Herold gave his name as "Smith" and according to Cobb, "...made use of a rather indelicate expression, and said he had been in bad company." Ibid., 252.

18 Forts Wagner and Baker were situated at the top of Good Hope Road in Uniontown. Booth and Herold probably passed between them shortly after eleven o'clock well in advance of any effort to alert the military forces to secure all avenues out of the city. The two fugitives were well ahead of the authorities who were still somewhat disorganized by the catastrophic events still unfolding back in the District. Fort Baker was in telegraphic communication with the military telegraph office, and around midnight began receiving messages from the military office in Washington. By that time Booth and Herold were out into Prince George's County, Maryland, and on the way to Surrattsville. See NARA, RG 393, Pt.2, 186.

19 For financial reasons, Mary Surratt decided to lease the tavern and move herself and young daughter Anna to the house she owned in Washington, D.C. Located at 541 H Street, within walking distance of Ford's Theatre, the house was used as a safe house for Confederate agents as well as a money-earning boarding house. Powell and Atzerodt stayed here at various times during the days leading up to that fateful Friday.

20 Gaddy, 129.

21 Mary Surratt made two visits to the tavern in early April 1865: the first on April 11 and the second on April 14, the day of the assassination. On April 14, she carried a package to Lloyd from Booth which later proved to be field glasses picked up by Booth later that night. During both of Mary Surratt's visits, John M. Lloyd testified that she had given him instructions to have ready items which would be picked up by persons later on. It was Lloyd's testimony along with Booth's numerous visits to the boarding house that convinced the members of the tribunal that Mary Surratt was an accomplice of Booth.

22 *Trial,* I:118.

23 Mary Surratt had met with Booth around noon on Friday and Booth asked her to take a small package to John Lloyd which proved to be a pair of field glasses. According to Lloyd, Mary Surratt also: "...told me to have those shooting-irons

ready that night, - there would be some parties call for them." Testimony of John M. Lloyd, *Trial*, I:118. It is this testimony in particular that sent Mary to the gallows.

24 Lloyd hid the second carbine in the tavern by carefully lowering it by an attached rope in the wall separating the kitchen from the dining room where it was found by soldiers searching the tavern.

25 *Trial*, I:119.

CHAPTER 4

1 Two statements were given by Mudd. The first statement, undated and referred to as Mudd's "voluntary" statement, was written in Mudd's own hand and given to Colonel H.H. Wells. The second statement was prepared by Wells on April 21 following his interview with Mudd, and was certified by Mudd with his signature, dated April 22, 1865. NARA, M-599, reel 5, frames 0212-0239. See Appendix 2.

2 In particular, Mudd claimed to have been anxious about a Confederate guerrilla who had frequented the area and whose demeanor was more that of a lawless renegade than that of a Southern freedom fighter. John H. Boyle, Jr. alias the Guerrilla Boyle, had appointed himself a Confederate enforcer in southern Maryland. He had murdered Union Captain Thomas W. Watkins on March 25, 1865 in his own home only three weeks prior to the loud knock on Mudd's door. See Hall, James O., "The Guerrilla Boyle," *The Maryland Independent*, May 7 and May 14, 1975, 1.

3 Voluntary Statement of Dr. S. A. Mudd. NARA, M-599, reel 5, frames 0226 through 0239. Reproduced by the Surratt Society. From *War Department Files. Statements Made By The Alleged Lincoln Conspirators Under Examination, 1865.* Surratt Society, 1980.

4 According to Mudd's statement he had three men as "working hands" on his farm, "two white and one colored." Mudd originally owned six slaves prior to Maryland's emancipation act in 1864.

5 On Tuesday, April 18, Lieutenant Alexander Lovett and his men visited the Mudd farm to question Dr. Mudd. Mudd was working in the field and while Lovett waited for him to return he questioned Francis Mudd, the doctor's wife. Mrs. Mudd stated that as the injured man and his friend were coming down the staircase to leave the house on Saturday afternoon (Dr. Mudd still being absent in Bryantown) she noticed the whiskers of the injured man seemed to come loose and fall away from one side of his face leading her to conclude that they were false whiskers. Testimony of Alexander Lovett, *Trial*, I:263. Also: NARA, War Department Records, file "L", R.B.P. 59, JAO.

6 Mr. Henson , according to Mudd's voluntary statement, was "... well acquainted through out the whole neighborhood," and again, "This young man mentioned the names of several parties in this neighborhood whom he knew, among others, several here in Bryantown. He mentioned being in the store of William Moore; he did not say when." Indeed, Davy Herold was very familiar with much of southern Maryland where he spent many days hunting and lounging about. He also was well acquainted with many of the residents of Charles County. Herold was familiar with Bryantown and knew how to get there from Mudd's, a fact which did not seem to spark Mudd's curiosity about the two strangers.

7 Parson Wilmer lived approximately five miles nearly due west of Mudd's farm. To reach Wilmer's house the two men would have to cross over the Zekiah Swamp.

8　"I first heard of the assassination of President Lincoln at Bryantown." Voluntary Statement of Dr. S. A. Mudd, NARA, M-599, reel 5, frames 0226-0239.

9　Lewis Powell in his attack on William Seward injured several other members of the household including Frederick Seward, Secretary Seward's second oldest son who served as assistant secretary of state. Frederick received several skull injuries from Powell's beating and was not expected to live. He eventually recovered, however, as did Seward and all the other injured members of his household.

10　*Trial*, III:418.

11　*Trial*, III:432. During the trial, Hardy testified that he had seen Booth on two separate occasions in the area: once at St. Mary's Church and a second time on the road near Bryantown. See *Trial*, III:433.

12　Dr. George Mudd (1826 - 1899) was a second cousin of Sam Mudd and lived less than a mile from Bryantown. Dr. Samuel Mudd passed by Dr. George Mudd's farm on both his trip to and from Bryantown the day before when he learned of Lincoln's assassination. Dr. George Mudd was known throughout the area as a Union sympathizer unlike his cousin. Like his cousin, he was a solid member in good standing in the surrounding community.

13　*Trial*, II:386.

14　Samuel Mudd's reluctance presumably stemmed from his fear of possible retribution by Confederate guerillas that might still be roaming the area.

15　*Trial*, II:391. This is the same group of soldiers that had been sent to Bryantown by General Augur as a result of John Fletcher's revelations earlier at army headquarters.

16　Lovett was accompanied by Detectives William Williams, Joshua Lloyd , Simon Gavacan, and several soldiers.

17　*Trial*, II:258.

18　Actually Booth was twenty-six years old and Davy Herold was two months shy of his twenty-third birthday (June 16, 1842).

19　Report of Lieutenant Alexander Lovett, NARA, M-619, reel 456, frames 0488 - 0490, AGO files.

20　David Herold gave the appearance of being much younger. Almost everyone described Herold as a boy or, at best, a young man who appeared to be a boy. Herold is frequently characterized by most writers as being "slow-witted" or acting simple at times. He actually was neither. Herold was clever enough to evade making serious mistakes during his interrogation on the monitor, *Montauk*, on April 27 and handled himself rather well. See NARA, M-599, reel 4, frame 0442 - 0485.

21　*Trial*, II:259. This may have been an attempt on Mudd's part to cover the delay in notifying the authorities until Monday, April 17.

22　*Trial*, II:261.

23　Booth purchased from his neighbor George Gardiner the one-eye horse which Powell rode the night of the assassination and which soldiers found roaming stray east of the capital. This was the horse wearing Atzerodt's saddle that was shown to John Fletcher at army headquarters between midnight and two a.m.

24　See Appendix 1.

25　Booth did not have a shawl at the theater or at the Surratt House. No mention of a shawl was made by John Lloyd in his testimony nor by Davy Herold in his testimony. If Booth had "a heavy shawl" when at Mudd's, where did he get it? Either he picked up the shawl at Dr. Mudd's house or Mudd fabricated the story of a shawl to support his claim that he did not recognize the injured man as Booth.

26 See Appendix 1.

27 When Booth entered the box at Ford's Theatre he carried a small derringer and a large bowie knife. The derringer (manufactured by Henry Deringer of Philadelphia and so marked) was recovered in the box early on the morning of April 15 by William F. Kent who turned it over to Lawrence Gobright, a member of the Associated Press. Gobright turned the derringer over to police chief A. C. Richards. See *Trial of John H. Surratt*, vol. I, Government Printing Office, 1866, p. 123. If Booth had two large revolvers as Mudd stated, he must have acquired them from Davy Herold after rendevousing with him at Soper's Hill or at Dr. Mudd's house. Both revolvers were recovered at the Garrett farm and are now in the Ford Theatre Museum.

28 See Appendix 1 for full statement.

29 Importantly, Booth had indelibly tattooed the initials "JWB" on the back of his left hand between the thumb and forefinger as a young boy. This distinctive marking was known by virtually everyone that was acquainted with the famous actor, and served as a positive identifying mark of Booth.

30 Statement of Mudd. NARA, M-599, reel 5, frames 0212 -0225.

31 Colonel and provost marshal, general defenses south of the Potomac.

CHAPTER 5

1 Mudd statement to Wells, NARA, M-599, reel 5, frames 0212-0225.

2 Louis J. Weichmann was an old schoolboy chum of John Surratt's and a boarder at Mary Surratt's boarding house in Washington. Weichmann became a key government witness who proved vital to the government's case supplying considerable detail about the comings and goings of John Surratt, Booth, and Mary Surratt highly reminiscent of John Dean's testimony a century later in the Watergate case. Weichmann has been criticized and occasionally vilified by supporters of Mary Surratt and Samuel Mudd as a liar and turncoat who turned state's witness to avoid prosecution. Weichmann's testimony, however, has held steadfast against considerable challenge. See *Trial*, I:69-110, I:135-136, I:369-390, II:42-44.

3 This memorandum detailing Booth's residency at the National Hotel in 1864 and 1865 was prepared by G. W. Bunker, the clerk of the National in anticipation of his testimony at the trial. Bunker's testimony covers the months of November and December, 1864. His testimony appears in *Trial*, I:29-32. The memoranda appears in, NARA, M-599, reel 15, frames 0262-0263. The actual register of the National Hotel is missing.

4 In the David Rankin Barbee papers housed in the Georgetown University Library is a letter written by John Wilkes Booth to J. Dominick Burch, proprietor of the tavern in Bryantown requesting Burch's help in retrieving an object (believed to be a pistol) which Booth left on the stage during his round trip. The letter is dated, Washington, November 14 (1864) further placing Booth in Washington on Monday the 14th.

5 Interview of Thomas Harbin by George Alfred Townsend, Cincinnati *Enquirer*, April 18, 1892.

6 Testimony of Thomas Gardiner, *Trial*, I:364.

7 The circumstances of this visit and the sequence of events was worked out by James O. Hall and appears in the book, *Come Retribution*. Hall originally misdated Booth's visit in December by three days, but in further research established Booth's visit between December 17 and December 22. Personal communication.

8   *Trial*, III:435.

9   Ibid.

10 Affidavit of Samuel A. Mudd dated August 28, 1865 in Laughlin, Clara, *The Death of Abraham Lincoln*, New York: Doubleday, Page & Company, 1909, 215-221. See Appendix 8.

11 See Appendix 7.

12 See Appendix 8.

13 Bunker memoranda.

14 Mudd had maintained that his only connection with Booth from the beginning was Booth's interest in purchasing land in Charles County. This was clearly a cover used by Booth and Mudd to explain their meetings.

15 *Trial*, II:258.

16 According to the testimony of Mary Simms, a former Mudd slave, John Surratt had visited the Mudd home on a dozen or more occasions and dined with Mudd in his home.

17 *Trial*, I:69-71.

18 In 1870, John Surratt gave a lengthy lecture at the courthouse in Rockville, Maryland in which he detailed his relationship with Booth and the events surrounding his involvement in the proposed capture of Lincoln. Surratt's *Rockville Lecture* is reprinted in its entirety in Weichmann, Louis J., *A True History of the Assassination of Abraham Lincoln and of the Conspiracy of 1865*, edited by Floyd E. Risvold, New York: Alfred A. Knopf, 1975, 428-440.

19 It appears that Jeremiah Mudd and Samuel Mudd separated for a period during the evening hours of December 23. The Pennsylvania House (also known as the Kimmel House) was where George Atzerodt bunked on his frequent visits to Washington and where he stayed the night of the assassination.

20 The time sequences and details for Booth's second visit to Charles County in December 1864 were worked out by James O. Hall.

CHAPTER 6

1   *Trial*, I:259.

2   Mudd Statement, NARA, M-599, reel 5, frames 0226-0239.

3   Mudd Statement, NARA, M-599, reel 5, frames 0226-0239.

4   Hardy testified that he had seen Booth in the Bryantown area on two separate occasions in November and December 1864. *Trial*, III:433.

5   *Trial*, III:420.

6   Mudd's role as a mail courier for the Confederacy is revealed by Samuel Cox, Jr. in his annotations of Thomas Jones' book, *J. Wilkes Booth*. Cox writes that the reason Mudd went into Bryantown on Saturday, April 15, was to mail letters he had, "...but a short time had gotten through the contraband mail for distribution...."

7   Jones' home, "Huckleberry," along with his farm is now a Catholic retreat known as "Loyola" operated by the Jesuit order.

8   Samuel Cox was not a colonel. He had briefly served as a captain of the local militia. The title of colonel was an honorary one among inhabitants of the region.

9   Statement of Oswell Swann, NARA, M-599, reel 6, frame 0227. Swann testified that Booth and Herold arrived at his cabin about nine p.m. and asked him to lead them to the home of William Burtles, a Confederate safehouse. Booth then changed his mind and instructed Swann to lead the two men to Samuel Cox's house for which they paid Swann twelve dollars.

10 Jones, Thomas A., *J. Wilkes Booth*. Laird & Lee, 1893. The book, long out of print, has been reprinted and may be obtained from the Surratt House Museum Gift Shop located in Clinton, Maryland.

11 Booth and Herold had been hidden in a pine thicket about one mile west of Cox's house by Cox's foreman, Frank Robey. Cox told Jones where to find the two fugitives. Jones, 73.

12 Booth's escape and eventual capture is detailed in: Steers, Edward, Jr. *The Escape and Capture of John Wilkes Booth*, Gettysburg: Thomas Publications, 1992.

13 Jones, 11.

14 Jones' book with Cox's annotations resides in The Maryland Historical Society. A photocopy of the annotations was obtained by James O. Hall. Photocopies were given by Mr. Hall to the writer and are quoted here.

15 According to Cox's annotations in the Jones book, mail drops were made in, "an old cedar stump on the knoll where E. J. Collis' house now stands...." This is well below Bryantown and would not be where Mudd would have dropped his mail. It is more likely that Mudd dropped his mail in Bryantown with the local postmaster who was also loyal to the Confederate cause.

16 In 1901 Osborn H. Oldroyd interviewed Samuel Cox, Jr. and was told the same account by Cox that appears in his annotations in Jones' book. Oldroyd published the account in his book, *Assassination of Abraham Lincoln*, privately published, Washington, D.C., 1901. See pages 265-269.

17 Pittman, Ben, *The Assassination of President Lincoln and the Trial of the Conspirators*, New York: Moore, Wilstach & Baldwin, 1865. See Appendix 7.

18 This affidavit also has Mudd acknowledging Booth's second visit to Charles County in December 1864, another fact he withheld from the authorities. See: Affidavit of Samuel A. Mudd in Laughlin, 215-220. See Appendix 2.

19 The Kimmel House or Pennsylvania Hotel was the same hotel where Mudd and his cousin stayed during their December, 1864 visit to Washington at the time Mudd introduced John Surratt to Booth. A stage coach line made a regular run between Washington and St. Mary's County stopping at the Kimmel House and the Bryantown Tavern.

20 Atzerodt's flight from Washington to the home of his cousin Hartman Richter and his subsequent capture is documented in the files of the NARA, M-619, reels 455 and 456. The documents appear in a pamphlet entitled *The Escape and Capture of George A. Atzerodt* by Edward Steers, Jr. and privately printed by the Surratt House Museum, Clinton, Maryland.

21 Hartranft Letters, Special Collections, Gettysburg College, Gettysburg, PA.

22 Atzerodt, *Lost Confession*.

23 Booth and Herold finally made the Virginia shore at a point where Gambo Creek empties into the Virginia side of the Potomac. Quesenberry's home was located a short distance from Gambo Creek on another creek by the name of Machodoc Creek.

24 Jones, 109-112.

25 Dr. Richard H. Stuart is the correct spelling. While the name is frequently spelled "Stewart" in the literature and in several of the original documents in the National Archives, "Stuart" is the spelling which appears on the doctor's tombstone at his home "Cedar Grove."

26 Statement of William Lucas, NARA, M-599, reel 5, frames 0144-0147.

27 Stuart was arrested on May 5 and imprisoned in the Old Capitol Prison in Washington. Released a month later, on June 7, Stuart returned home escaping the retribution that fell on several others.

28 Statement of Richard Stuart, NARA, M-599, reel 6, frames 0205-0211.

29 Ibid., (NARA, May 6, 1865).

30 Statement of William L. Bryant, NARA, M-519, reel 4, frame 0095. The correct spelling is Stuart. The spelling Stuart, suggests the statement was taken down by sound, and not written down by Bryant.

CHAPTER 7

1   The defendants included in the charges along with Mudd were, David E. Herold, George A. Atzerodt, Lewis Powell, Michael O'Laughlen, Edward Spangler, Samuel Arnold and Mary E. Surratt. Absent from this group was John H. Surratt (missing) and John Wilkes Booth (dead).

2   *Trial*, I:19.

3   *History Rewritten: The Case of Dr. Samuel A. Mudd,* written and directed by Paul Davis and produced by Fedoruk, Light Vision Films, 1995. This eighty minute video tape does an excellent job in presenting the case of Dr. Mudd from the perspective of his advocates. Copies of this video are available from the Surratt House Museum Gift Shop, Clinton, Maryland.

4   Mudd, Nettie, *The Life of Dr. Samuel A. Mudd,* New York and Washington: Neale Publishing Company, 1906, 131-132. Reprint. Linden, TN: Continental Book Company, 1975.

5   Ibid., 350.

6   Ibid., 144.

7   Mudd Voluntary Statement, NARA, M-599, reel 5, frames 0226 - 0239.

8   Letter from Mudd to O. A. Brownson (original in O. A. Brownson collection, University of Notre Dame Archives), reproduced in Mudd, Nettie.

9   Booth kept an incriminating letter written by Samuel Arnold in his personal belongings which resulted in Arnold being convicted, and he planted his bank book in Atzerodt's room at the Kirkwood implicating him. Booth also visited the Kirkwood earlier on Friday, April 14, leaving a personal card for Andrew Johnson in an effort to implicate Johnson should Atzerodt fail as Booth suspected he might. If Booth went down, he fully expected to take others with him including Mary Surratt and John Surratt.

10 Samuel Cox, Jr., in his annotations in Thomas Jones' book, quoted Mudd as telling him, "... and now the third time, (Booth) had come with a lie upon his tongue...." This further supports the fact that Booth had visited Mudd twice before at his home and not once as Mudd previously claimed.

11 William Burtles owned a house to the east of Mudd's which served as a safe house for Confederate operatives. Booth and Herold started out for Burtles' but got lost and came across Oswell Swann who they then asked to lead them to Samuel Cox's plantation instead.

12 Lieutenant Mortimer B. Ruggles, Private Absalom Bainbridge and Private Willie Jett. The three Confederate soldiers had recently been disbanded from Mosby's command and met Booth and Herold on Monday morning on the northern side of the Rappahannock River. Willie Jett took Booth to the farm of Richard Garrett. Herold went on to Bowling Green with the three soldiers and then to the home of Joseph Clarke where he spent the night. Herold returned to the Garrett farm on the afternoon of April 25 where he stayed with Booth until members of the 16th New York Cavalry arrived early Wednesday morning, April 26.

13 *Trial*, III, 433.

CHAPTER 8

1 Lincoln, *Works*, 518-537. Lincoln used this phrase in his Annual Message to Congress (37th Congress, third session) on December 1, 1862.

2 Weckesser, Elden C., *His Name Was Mudd*, North Carolina and London: McFarland & Company, Inc., Publishers, 1991, 199.

3 Mudd escaped the gallows by a single vote. The tribunal voted to hang Mudd five votes to four, but a hanging sentence required a two-thirds majority or six votes.

4 Mudd must bear responsibility for bringing Thomas Harbin and John H. Surratt into Booth's conspiracy. It was Dr. Mudd who specifically made the introductions of these two key members of the abduction conspiracy to Booth at prearranged meetings and it was John Surratt's participation that tied his mother, Mary Surratt, into the conspiracy. Without Mudd's active role and presumed credibility with Harbin and Surratt, they might never have agreed to join in Booth's plot and Mary Surratt and the three other men with her would not have wound up on the gallows.

5 Mudd, Nettie.

6 *Rewriting History: The Case of Dr. Samuel Mudd.*

7 McHale, John E., Jr., *Dr. Samuel A. Mudd and the Lincoln Assassination*, Parsippany, NJ: Dillon Press, 1995, 43-45.

8 Weckesser, 69.

9 Hartranft Letters, Gettysburg College Library, Gettysburg, PA. Photocopies in the files of James O. Hall.

10 McHale. Dr. Richard D. Mudd holds a Master's Degree in sociology, a PhD in history, and a doctorate in medicine from Georgetown University.

11 Ibid. There have been numerous gestures over the years by various bodies to honor or at least acknowledge Dr. Samuel A. Mudd and reverse the perception of his guilt. In 1961, a special plaque was affixed at Fort Jefferson honoring the doctor's efforts in the yellow fever epidemic. Several political bodies have passed resolutions in support of Mudd's innocence and even an elementary school and hospital room have been named after him.

12 Personal communication from Dr. Richard D. Mudd.

13 Letter from President Jimmy Carter to Dr. Richard D. Mudd, July 24, 1979, in the possession of Dr. Richard D. Mudd.

14 See appendix 4.

15 Jones, John Paul, ed., *Dr. Mudd and the Lincoln Assassination. The Case Reopened.* Conshohocken, PA: Combined Books, 1995.

16 This is discussed fully in Chapter Nine.

17 As discussed in Chapter Nine, Mudd was afforded full due process in the courts following his conviction. He appealed his case to the federal court for the Southern District of Florida where it was denied. The case was then appealed to the Supreme Court of the United States where arguments were heard, but the petition was dismissed before an opinion could be issued as the plaintiffs were pardoned by President Johnson making the petition moot. Mudd was not denied his rights in the American judicial system as most claim.

18 Jones, 274.

19 Also presenting the case for Dr. Mudd was the well-known defense attorney, F. Lee Bailey. Representing the military commission were John Jay Douglass, dean of the National College of District Attorneys and professor of law, University of Houston Law Center, former commandant of the Judge Advocate General's School and past president of the Army Judge Advocates Association; and John S. Jenkins, associate dean and lecturer, George Washington Univer-

sity National Law Center, former judge advocate general of the Navy and special counsel to the secretary of the Navy.

20 Two excellent articles discussing Mudd's guilt may be found in Jones: *The Curious Case of Dr. Mudd*, by Forest J. Bowman, and *The Case Against Dr. Samuel Mudd: Why His Family's Vanity Does Not Justify Rewriting Dr. Mudd's Story*, by Andrew C. Carington and Floyd E. Risvold.

21 Jones, 117-251.

22 See Appendix 11 for Congressman Hoyer's remarks from the floor of the House, and the complete text of the bill H.R. 1885.

23 U.S. Congress, House, Committee on National Security, Subcommittee on Military Personnel, *To direct the Secretary of the Army to set aside the conviction of Dr. Samuel A. Mudd by a military commission in 1865 for aiding, abetting, and assissting the conspirators who assassinated...*, 105th Cong., 1st Sess., 12 June, 1997.

24 Ibid., Section 2., paragraphs 1 and 2.

25 James O. Hall, letter to Angela Breeck, editor, *Maryland Independent*, 15 July, 1997, author's files.

26 And, for that matter, for John H. Surratt and Mary E. Surratt.

CHAPTER 9

1 The farm house which Dr. Mudd would purchase was built in 1830 and had become known as the Rock Hill Farm by the time Mudd acquired it.

2 Mudd, Nettie.

3 Jeremiah (Jere) Dyer would later marry Samuel Mudd's sister, Mary Clare Mudd, in 1867 while Mudd was still a prisoner at Fort Jefferson in the Dry Tortugas.

4 Weckesser.

5 Thomas Dyer Mudd was the father of Dr. Richard Dyer Mudd of Saginaw Michigan. Dr. Richard Mudd has mounted a considerable effort for over seventy years to reverse the judgment of the military tribunal and exonerate his grandfather.

6 Mary Simms, Elzee Eglent, Sylvester Eglent, Melvina Washington, Milo Simms and Rachel Spencer. See *Trial*, II:150,157,159,163,170 and 341.

7 Among the men identified was Captain Walter "Watt" Bowie, a prominent Prince George's County dignitary who rode with the famous Colonel John Mosby. Bowie was shot and killed after a raid near Rockville, Maryland in May 1864 referred to by local residents as the Battle of Rickett's Run.

8 *Trial*, II:157.

9 *Trial*, II: 154.

10 Weckesser, 125.

11 McHale, 79.

12 Mudd, Nettie, 128.

13 McHale, 93.

14 A description of these items may be found in the newsletters published by the Dr. Samuel A. Mudd Society entitled, *The Committee for the Restoration of the Dr. Samuel A. Mudd House, Inc.*, Vol. 1, No.8 and Vol. 1, No. 9, September, 1980 and December, 1980 respectively.

15 In 1936, John Houston directed the movie, *Prisoner of Shark Island* starring Warner Baxter based on the life of Dr. Mudd as seen through the eyes of Hollywood. While the movie was an historical farce, it elevated Dr. Mudd to a new folk hero status, truly the victim of a hysterical and brutal United States government that turned Fort Jefferson (Shark Island) into a "Devil's Island" for the sole purpose of torturing Dr. Mudd. In the movie, Dr. Mudd is not seen fashioning cabinetry at any time.

16   McHale, 102-114. Weckesser, 174-188.

17   The pardon is dated February 8, 1869. Mudd received official notification at Fort Jefferson thirty days later on March 8, 1869.

18   Arnold returned to his home in Baltimore and lived out his years in relative peace pausing only to write a book about his experiences. He died in 1906. Spangler returned to his old employer John T. Ford and eventually made his way to the home of Dr. Mudd in 1873 where he lived out the remainder of his years until his death in 1875. He was buried by Dr. Mudd in the old St. Peter's Cemetery across the road from the Mudd church. The grave was unmarked and remained so until 1985 when a joint effort of the Surratt Society and Dr. Samuel A. Mudd Society placed a gravestone on the alleged site.

19   Henry, 1870; Stella Marie, 1871; Edward Joseph, 1873; Rose De Lima, 1875; and Mary Eleanor (Nettie), 1878.

CHAPTER 10

1   This chapter is taken from an earlier version which appeared in the *Lincoln Herald* as Steers, Edward, Jr., "Inter Arma Silent Leges," *Lincoln Herald*, 83: No. 3, 719-730, fall, 1981.
"The law is silent among arms." This ominous maxim is taken from Attorney General James Speed's opinion provided to President Andrew Johnson dated July 1865. Speed maintained that this dictum was never wholly true as the object of the laws of war was to limit, as much as possible, injury to persons and property during war. See Speed, James F., *Opinion on the Constitutional Power of the Military to Try and Execute the Assassins of the President*, Government Printing Office, Washington, D.C. July, 1865.

2   Surratt was in Canada where he had been enroute on a mission for the Confederacy when Lincoln was assassinated. Friends quickly hid him and provided for him while the manhunt and subsequent trial took place. He eventually made his way to Europe, then the Vatican, where he briefly served as a Papal guard before being discovered. Taken into custody, he made a miraculous escape and sailed for Egypt only to be captured by United States authorities in Alexandria. He was returned to the United States where he was tried in civil court as a conspirator in Lincoln's murder. The jury failed to reach a verdict and Surratt was released when the government decided not to seek a new trial.

3   Interestingly, the original order is written in Secretary of War Edwin Stanton's own hand on War Department stationary. Stanton obviously made the decision to try the accused before a military court and drafted the executive order for Johnson to sign.

4   *Trial*, I:5.

5   War Department circular dated April 20, 1865. See Fleet, Betsy, "A Chapter of Unwritten History: Richard Bayard Garrett's Account of the Flight and Death of John Wilkes Booth." *The Virginia Magazine*, No. 4:387, 1963, 71. Also, Weckesser.

6   *Ex parte Milligan*, 4 Wall. 2:18 L.Ed. 281.

7   Arnold and Spangler filed a petition of habeas corpus with the Supreme Court in February 1869 as a result of their petition before the United States District Court of Southern Florida being denied. The Supreme Court agreed to hear the case and arguments were made before it by lawyers for the plaintiffs and the government. Andrew Johnson pardoned the two plaintiffs on March 1, 1869, and according to the court's calendar dated March 19, 1869, Chief Justice Salmon P. Chase dismissed the petition without a court ruling leaving the petition moot. For a full discussion of the hearing before the U.S. District Court for the Southern District of

Florida and the filing with the United States Supreme Court, see James E. T. Lange and Katharine DeWitt, Jr., "Mudd Habeas Corpus," *Surratt Courier*, 19, no. 1 (1994): 5-7.

8   Basler, Roy P., Marion D. Pratt, and Lloyd A. Dunlap, *The Collected Works of Abraham Lincoln*, 9 Volumes, New Brunswick, NJ: 1953, **IV**:344.

9   Lincoln, *Works*, **IV**:347.

10 The applicable clause is found in Article I, Section 9, paragraph 2 of the Constitution of the United States.

11 During this period in history justices of the Supreme Court served on circuit court duty while the Supreme Court was in recess. Chief Justice Taney received the Merryman petition while sitting as circuit court judge for the District of Baltimore during the April 1861 term. Taney's opinion is published in 17 Fed.Case 144.

12 Lincoln, *Works*, **IV**:344, 347, 364, 414, and Lincoln, *Works* supplement, 1832-1865, 109, 1974.

13 Lincoln, *Works*, **V**:436-437.

14 Neely, Mark E., *The Fate of Liberty*, New York: Oxford University Press, 1991. Neely, in a meticulous study of martial law and military commissions, concluded that such trials , "...were marked by procedural regularity," and that Judge Advocate General Joseph Holt was, "... a punctilious lawyer and military administrator who repeatedly overturned the decisions of trials by military commission (as well as courts-martial) for what can only be called legal technicalities." See Neely, 162.   While military justice in regard to civilians may have been viewed as harsh, Neely, in reviewing one hundred and eighty-four cases involving the death sentence which were sent to Lincoln between 1863 and 1865 for his approval, observed that Lincoln mitigated the punishment in eighty-nine of the cases or nearly one-half. See Neely, 165-166.

15 Copperhead was the name given to those Northern Democrats who actively supported the Confederate cause. While some merely believed in the right of a state to secede, others were more active in supporting (and even supplying) the Confederacy in word and deed.

16 *Ex parte Vallandigham*, 1 Wall. 243.

17 Pittman, *Trial*, 2.

18 Interestingly, the original draft of the Executive Order signed by Johnson is written in Stanton's own hand and appears on War Department stationary suggesting that Secretary of War Stanton was the originator of trying the accused before a military commission. While Stanton may have orchestrated the use of a military trial, there is no evidence that he orchestrated James Speed's opinion.

19 Speed, *Opinion*, 8.

20 *Ex parte Vallandigham*, 1 Wall. 243.

21 Speed, *Opinion*, 15.

22 Ibid.

23 Martial law came into effect throughout the United States for certain individuals and situations as a result of Lincoln's proclamation of September 24, 1862. The conditions of this proclamation were still in force at the time of Lincoln's assassination and the trial of the conspirators. Martial law was revoked by Andrew Johnson only after the trial and execution had taken place.

24 *Ex parte Milligan*, 4 Wall. 2, 18 L.Ed. 281.

25 Arrested with Milligan and tried by the military tribunal were William A. Bowles, Andrew Humphreys, Horace Heffren and Stephen Horsey.

26 According to Stanton biographer Frank A. Flower, Milligan's wife, who was an old childhood friend of Edwin Stanton, carried Milligan's written brief to Stanton

and pleaded for her husband's life. Stanton accepted Milligan's brief and told Mrs. Milligan that her husband would not be executed. Within hours, Governor Morton of Indiana received a dispatch from the War Department commuting the sentence. See, Flowers, Frank A., *Edwin McMasters Stanton*, New York: The Saalfield Publishing Company, 1906.

27 In a five to four vote the Court also ruled that the Congress had no power under the Constitution to authorize a military commission. The dissenting opinion, given by Chief Justice Salmon P. Chase, maintained that the war powers granted Congress authorized it to enact legislation establishing military commissions.

28 The question of Lincoln's suspension of the writ of habeas corpus became a moot point as a result of Congress' Act of March 1863, authorizing such suspension.

29 King, Willard L. *Lincoln's Manager David Davis*. Cambridge, MA: Harvard University Press, 263.

30 Salmon P. Chase papers, Department of History, Claremont Graduate School, Claremont, California.

31 The Court's records are missing, but the complete Boynton opinion may be found in a newspaper (unidentified) clipping in the *Lincoln Obsequies Scrapbook* located in the Library of Congress, Manuscript Division. The article purports to be a verbatim transcript of the opinion filed by Boynton for the United States District of Florida. The original case is cited in: 17 Fed. Case, 954. For a further discussion of Mudd's petition see Gary R. Planck, "Lincoln's Assassination: More "Forgotten" Litigation - ex parte Mudd (1868)," Lincoln *Herald*, 76, No. 2, 86-90, 1974.

32 The court's records are missing, but the complete Boynton opinion was discovered by James O. Hall in a newspaper (unidentified) clipping in the *Lincoln Obsequies Scrapbook* located in the Library of Congress, Manuscript Division. The article purports to be a verbatim transcript of the opinion filed by Boynton for the United States District of Florida. Subsequently the verbatim transcript of the case was published in the *Surratt Courier*. See James E. T. Lange and Katherine DeWitt, J., "Ex Parte Mudd Confirmed," *Surratt Courier*, 21, no. 3, (1996) pp. 4-8. The original case is cited in: 17 Fed.case, 954. For a further discussion of Mudd's petition see Gary R. Planck, "Lincoln's Assassination: More "Forgotten" Litigation—ex parte Mudd (18868)." *Lincoln Herald*, 76, no. 2, pp. 86-90 (1974).

33 The eleven Southern states were divided into five military districts along the following lines: West Virginia, Virginia; North and South Carolina; Georgia, Alabama, Florida; Mississippi and Arkansas; and Louisiana and Texas.

34 *Ex parte Garland*, 4 Wall. 333; Cummings vs, Missouri, 4 Wall. 277.

35 *Ex parte McCardle*, 6 Wall. 318.

36 *Ex parte McCardle*, 7 Wall. 506.

37 The eight consisted of Richard Quirin, George Dasch, Ernest Burger, Heinrich Heinck, Edward Kerling, Hermann Neubauer, Herbert Haupt and Werner Thiel. All eight saboteurs had lived in the United States previously and all eight spoke fluent English. Two of the eight were U. S. citizens. By June 27, 1942, they were standing trial before a military tribunal ordered by President Franklin Roosevelt. Leading the defense was army appointed counsel Colonel Robert Royall who promptly petitioned the Supreme Court for a writ of habeas corpus.

38 Proclamation No. 2561, July 2, 1942. 7 F.R. 5101, 56 Stat., 1964, "Enemies denied access to United States Courts," 10 U.S.C. 906.

39 *Ex parte Quirin*, 317, U.S. 1.
40 On August 3, 1942, the commission found the defendants guilty on all charges, and on August 8, all but Dasch and Burger were electrocuted in the District of Columbia jail. Dasch and Burger, who told everything to the FBI, received jail terms which were to be commuted to deportation at the end of the war.
41 *Ex parte Yamashita*, 327 U.S. 1.
42 The establishment of martial law over the domestic population as it existed during the Civil War did not end as a result of the Supreme Court ruling in *ex parte Milligan*. Shortly after the Japanese attack on Pearl Harbor in 1941, the governor of the Territory of Hawaii closed the civil courts and turned the government over to the commanding general of the department with the full approval of the president of the United States. Two years later, in February, 1944, the Supreme Court again invoked *ex parte Milligan* in ruling that martial law can only exist when the civil arm of the government becomes powerless because of invasion, insurrection or anarchy. Duncan v. Kahanamoku, 327 U.S. 304.
43 Powell served as a private in Mosby's command while O'Laughlen and Arnold served in the First Maryland Infantry; O'Laughlen in Company D, and Arnold in Company C. See John C. Brennan, "Bradley T. Johnson's Plan to Abduct President Lincoln," *Chronicles of St. Mary's*, vol. 22, no. 12, December, 1974. 421-425.

APPENDIX 6

1 Atzerodt, *Lost Confession*. See note 21, Chapter 2.
2 James Wood was an alias used by Lewis Powell. While boarding at the Surratt House, Powell represented himself as a Baptist minister which came naturally to him as his father was, in fact, a Baptist minister.
3 Louis J. Weichmann, a classmate and boyhood friend of John H. Surratt, Jr., boarded at the Surratt boarding house in Washington. He became an important witness for the government's case against John and Mary Surratt.
4 Thomas Harbin was a member of the Confederate Signal Service (Secret Service) and in charge of Virginia's north shore of the Potomac River. Mudd arranged a meeting between Harbin and Booth in December 1864, at Bryantown.
5 John Boyle, known locally as the Guerrilla Boyle, sometimes terrorized the area of Prince George's County and Charles County. Mudd claims that he first thought it was Boyle who banged on his door early Saturday morning when Booth and Herold arrived. The government at first thought it was Boyle who had attacked Seward on Friday evening. The truth is, Mudd nothing to fear from Boyle.
6 John H. Caldwell managed the grocery store of Matthews and Company in Georgetown. Matthews was a wholesale and retail dealer in "fine teas and choice groceries for the family." Atzerodt stopped here early Saturday morning while fleeing Washington. He pawned his revolver with Caldwell for $10.00 before proceeding on to the home of his cousin, Hartman Richter in Germantown, Montgomery County, Maryland where he was eventually captured early Thursday morning, April 20.

APPENDIX 9

1 NARA, M-619, reel 456, frames 0488 - 0490.

INDEX

The names of each of the major conspirators involved with John Wilkes Booth occur frequently throughout the text. Therefore, John Wilkes Booth, Samuel Arnold, George A. Atzerodt, Thomas Harbin, David Herold, Dr. Samuel A. Mudd, Michael O'Laughlen, Lewis Powell, Edman Spangler, John H. Surratt, Jr., and Mary Surratt are not listed in this index.

-A-

ABCMR, 78, 79, 81
Act of February, 1867, 100
Allen's Fresh, Md., 20
Army of Northern Virginia, 15
Army of the Shenandoah, 15
Army of the Valley, 13
Atlanta, Ga., 13
Augur, Christopher Columbus, 8, 9

-B-

Baltimore, Md., 91
Baltimore Medical College, 82, 83
Beantown, Md., 24
Bingham, Judge Advocate John A., 50
Black, Jeremiah S., 96
Booth, Edwin, 64
Boynton, Thomas Jefferson, 79, 98, 99, 104
Brownson, Orestes A., 65, 66, 72, 84
Brownson's Quarterly Review, 65
Bryant, William, 57, 59, 62
Bryantown, Md., 9, 20, 29, 30, 33, 35, 37, 40, 44, 49, 50, 54, 61-63
Bryantown Tavern, 31, 40, 53, 57, 61
Buckner, General Simon Bolivar, CSA, 10
Burroughs, "Peanuts," 22, 24
Burtles, William, 68
Butler, Benjamin F., 96

-C-

Cadwallader, Maj. General George B., USA, 92
Campbell Hospital, 16
Capitol Prison (Carroll Annex), 38, 53
Carter, Jimmy, 1-3, 76-78
Chase, Salmon P., 98
Clark, William D., 79
Cobb, Silas T., 5, 8, 24, 26, 68

Confederate Secret Service, 13, 72
copperhead, 93
Cox, Samuel, Jr., 50, 52, 54, 55, 61-63, 67, 72, 88

-D-

Dana, Lt. David D., USA, 9, 31
Davenport, E. L., 16
Davis, David, 95, 96, 98
Davis, Jefferson, 11, 13, 18, 60, 68
Doster, Capt. William E., USA, 56
Dry Tortugas, 44, 55, 73, 84, 98
Dutton, Capt. George W., USA, 44, 55, 62
Dyer, Jeremiah, 83, 85

-E-

Early, Maj. General Jubal, CSA, 13, 15
Eglen, Elzee, 83
Ewing, Jr., Brig. General Thomas, USA, 80
Ewing, Thomas, Rep., 80
ex parte Milligan, 90, 95, 97-103
ex parte Quirin, 101, 103

-F-

Farrell, Francis, 30, 49, 50, 61, 62
Field, David Dudley, 96
Field, Stephen S., 96
Fletcher, John, 4, 5, 8, 9, 21, 24, 26
Forbes, Charles, 22
Ford, Harry Clay, 17
Ford's Theatre, 8, 9, 15, 17, 21, 55, 73
Forrest, General Nathan Bedford, CSA, 10
Fort Donelson, Tn., 10, 11
Fort Jefferson, Fl., 43, 55, 73, 84, 90
Fort McHenry, Md., 91, 92
Frank Leslie's Magazine, 76
Frederick, Md., 13, 82, 83

-G-

Gardiner, George, 35, 38, 40, 42, 61
Garfield, James A., 96
Garrett Farm, 57, 69
Garrett, Richard, 38
Gavacan, Simon, 34
Georgetown College (University), 82
Germantown, Md., 56
Grant, General Ulysses S., USA, 10, 15, 17

-H-

H. R. 1885, 81
habeas corpus, writ of, 91-93, 95-97, 99-101
Hall, James O., 3, 54, 81
Hampton, Maj. General Wade, CSA, 13
Hancock, Maj. General Winfield Scott, USA, 74, 76
Hardy, John F., 30, 35, 42, 45, 50, 61, 62, 69
Harris, Clara, 22, 24
Hartranft, Maj. General John F., USA, 74-76
Henry, Michael, 9
Herndon House, 21
Holt, Brig. General Joseph, USA, 44
Horse Head Road, 43, 45
Hovey, Maj. General Alvin P., USA, 95
Hoyer, Steny, 80, 81
Hughes, John J., 53
Hunter, Maj. General David, USA, 15

-J-

Johnson, Andrew, 1, 2, 5, 9, 16, 21, 55, 76, 77, 88, 93, 94, 96-100, 102
Johnson, Bradley T., CSA, 13, 15, 18
Johnston, Col. William Preston, CSA, 11
Jones, Thomas A., 50, 52-54, 68, 72
Judicial Act of 1789, 93

-K-

Keene, Laura, 17
Kimmel House, 55
King George County, Va., 20
Kirkwood Hotel, 5, 9, 16, 21, 55

-L-

Lee, General Robert E., CSA, 15
Lee, John, 9

Lincoln Hospital, 8
Lincoln, Mary Todd, 17
Lloyd, John M., 26
Lloyd, Joshua, 34
Lovett, Lt. Alexander, 33-35, 38, 49, 68

-M-

martial law, 92, 95, 97, 99, 101
Maryland Independent, 81
Mathias Point, Va., 20
McCardle, William C., 100
McDonald, David, 95, 96
McPhail, James L., 56
Merryman, John B., 91, 92
Mexican War, 92, 93
Milligan, Lambdin P., 90, 95, 96
Morton, Oliver P., 96
Mudd, Andrew Jerome, 83
Mudd, George, 30-34, 49, 63, 82, 84
Mudd, Henry Lowe, Sr., 29, 82
Mudd, Jeremiah T., 45
Mudd, Lillian Augusta, 83
Mudd, Nettie, 73
Mudd, Richard Dyer, 1, 2, 3, 76-78
Mudd, Roger, 1
Mudd, Samuel Alexander II, 83
Mudd, Sarah Frances Dyer (Frank), 28, 34, 35, 69, 82, 88
Mudd, Thomas Dyer, 83

-N-

Nanjemoy Creek, 53
National Hotel, 16, 40, 42, 44, 45, 61
National Theatre, 16, 17
Navy Yard, 55
Navy Yard Bridge, 5, 8, 9, 21, 24, 68
Naylor, Thompson, 5
New York Cavalry (13th), 9, 30, 31
Newport, Md., 20

-O-

Oak Hill, 29, 82
O'Beirne, Major James, USA, 9
Ord, Maj. General E. O. C., USA, 100
Order of the Sons of Liberty, 95

-P-

Pennsylvania House, 47, 55
Piney Church, 30, 34, 50, 59
Point of Rocks, Md., 15

Port Royal, Va., 38
Proclamation of 1862, 97

-Q-
Queen, Dr. William, 38, 40, 72
Quesenberry, Elizabeth, 56

-R-
Radical Republicans, 99, 100
Rathbone, Maj. Henry, 22, 24
Reagan, Ronald, 1, 3, 78
Reconstruction Act, 99, 100
Rich Hill, 50, 52, 54
Richmond, Va., 11, 16, 18, 20, 26, 44
Richter, Hartman, 56
Rockville Lecture, 47
Rockville, Md., 56
Roosevelt, Franklin D., 1, 76, 101

-S-
St. Catharine's, 83
St. John's College, Frederick, Md., 82
St. Mary's Catholic Church, 35, 40, 42,
   45, 61, 64, 69, 72, 88
St. Peter's Church, 30, 49, 69
Scott, General Winfield, 91-93
Seward, Frederick, 30
Seward, William, 4, 21, 30
Shark Island, 73, 75
Shenandoah Valley, 13, 15
Shepherdstown, W. Va., 15
Sheridan, Maj. General Philip, USA, 15
Smith, Dr. Joseph Sim, 85, 88
Smith, John L., 56
Soldiers' Home, 11, 13, 15
Soper's Hill, Md., 21
Speed, James, 79, 94, 101, 102, 104
Stanton, Edwin M., 18, 26, 74, 84, 95
Star Saloon, 22
Stone, Charles, 8
Stuart, Dr. Richard, 57, 59, 62, 67, 68
Surratt, John H. Sr., 26

Surratt Tavern, 20
Surrattsville, Md., 26
Swann, Oswell (Oswald), 50, 68

-T-
Taney, Roger Brook, 91-93
Taylor, General Joseph, USA, 10
Taylor, Maj. Joseph Walker, CSA, 10,
   11, 13, 18
Taylor, Maj. General Richard, CSA, 10
Taylor, Sarah Knox, 10
Taylor, Zachary, 10
Thompson, John, 35, 38, 72

-U-
Union Hotel, 5
Uniontown, Md., 5, 8
University of Richmond School of Law,
   79

-V-
Vallandigham, Clement L., 93, 94, 103

-W-
Washington Arsenal, 38, 56, 74
Washington Navy Yard, 5
Washington Penitentiary, 74
Weichmann, Louis J., 40, 44, 45, 47
Wells, Col. H. H., 33, 35-38, 68, 89
White Plains, Md., 5
Whitehurst, Dr. D. W., 88
White's Ford, Md., 13
Williams, William, 34
Williamsport, Md., 15
Wilmer, Rev., 29, 30, 34, 50, 59, 68

-Y-
Yamashita, Japanese General
   Tomoyuki, 102, 103

-Z-
Zekiah Swamp, 30, 34, 50, 68, 89